MW01230678

TAY
The Taylor Swift Story

Proof editor: Michele Caterina
Cover photos ©   front: Reuters/Danny Moloshok
                      back: Reuters/Lucas Jackson
Cover design: Omer Pikarsky
Inside page layout: Lazar Kackarovski

Library of Congress Cataloging-in-Publication data available.

ISBN : 978-1-938591-31-0

Published by Sole Books, Beverly Hills, California.

Printed in the United States of America

Second edition April 2019

10987654321

www.solebooks.com

tay
The Taylor Swift Story

Jill Parker

Sole
BOOKS

To Mikaela Long
Vine artist and die-hard Swiftie

ONE

"Someday I'm gonna sing in there," Taylor said, staring out the side window of the Swift family Jeep Wagoneer at the Bluebird Café as they drove by.

"But that's a bar," Andrea Swift, Taylor's mother said, driving.

"So? Leann Rimes sang in there. If it's good enough for her, it's good enough for me."

"Whatever you say, Tay," Andrea said and continued driving.

Taylor stared out the side window as her mother drove slowly down Music Row in Nashville, Tennessee. They were looking for record companies with names Taylor recognized. She sat beside her mother in the front seat and her younger brother, Austin, had the backseat all to himself. She had a half-full box of demo CDs with her picture on it and the words, *CALL ME,* boldly printed under her headshot that was taken by her neighbor at their Christmas tree farm. On the album cover, she had dressed herself as a country singer in a blouse and skirt and cowboy boots. Her long white-blonde mane of unruly hair blew in wings across her face in the photo, just as they did now while they drove.

Music Row, on Commerce Street in the heart of Nashville, was where all the record companies set up shop. They had already stopped at nineteen companies and Taylor had personally left a demo at each stop. Unfortunately, that was nineteen record companies and nineteen rejections. But this did not discourage her. It hurt on the inside, but she was not going to show it and she was not going to give up. She did not wait all eleven, almost twelve, years of her life to bail on her dreams just because a few record companies did not see what she saw.

Then she saw it. And screamed.

Andrea, terrified at her daughter's scream, slammed on the brakes and the car skidded to a stop in the middle of traffic.

Horns blared.

"I swear, Taylor, you almost scared the life out of me!" Andrea said.

"Look!" Taylor said, pointing at the building with UMG on the side of it, along with MCA and Mercury Records.

It was Reba McEntire and George Strait's label. Andrea sighed. "I think we just found number twenty." She quickly eased the Wagoneer to the curb just past the building.

Taylor unbuckled her seat belt. She grabbed a single CD jewel case from a stack resting on the center console. Besides the headshot and CALL ME on the front, on the back was her Pennsylvania telephone number, her email address, and a short list of cover songs she sang to karaoke background music.

She turned to her mother. "I've got a good feeling about this," she said.

"Not me!" eight-year-old Austin shouted from the backseat. "I want to go home!"

"Soon," Andrea said. "Hold your horses."

They all laughed and Taylor gave her little brother a look, and he scrunched down in his seat.

Taylor threw open the passenger door and got out, slammed the door shut, walked slowly and carefully, and counted every step. Her mother and brother followed close behind. Andrea never let Taylor go up to a label alone.

The building got closer and Taylor's heart raced. Just like all the other times. She was kind of used to it after nineteen stops, but she just could not contain her excitement. She started skipping to get to the building quicker. When she got to the front door, her mom and brother were right behind her. She kissed her mom on the cheek. "For luck," she said.

Back in Wyomissing, Pennsylvania, Taylor had recorded four songs, backed up by canned karaoke music. She could not afford a band and she couldn't play any instruments. It was okay. She loved karaoke.

She sang "Here You Come Again," originally recorded by Dolly Parton, "There's Your Trouble" by The Dixie Chicks, and "One Way Ticket" by LeAnn Rimes.

LeAnn Rimes was her hero, not only because she sang a mean country tune, but also because she made it big at age 13. The fourth song was "Hopelessly Devoted" by Olivia Newton-John. It was her favorite song from *Grease,* a play Taylor did the year before. She took in a deep breath and went inside.

In the lobby, Taylor marched up to the woman behind the front desk. And when she looked up from her paperwork, Taylor went into gear. "Hi! I'm Taylor Swift! I'm eleven and I want a record deal!" She handed the woman her CD. "Call me!" she said and flashed her a cheery smile.

The receptionist smiled. "Well, aren't you a cutie," she said. "But we don't make record deals with anyone under eighteen. You know why? 'Cuz kids don't listen to country."

"LeAnn Rimes was number one when she was thirteen," Taylor countered.

The woman chuckled. "Well, you got me there, sweetie," she said. "Your telephone number on this?"

"Yes, ma'am," Taylor said. "All right, we'll be in touch." "Really?"

The woman behind the desk took a deep breath, then gave her a weary, disappointed look. "You never know."

Taylor bit her lip and turned and raced out, letting the door close behind her.

The woman behind the desk watched her go, then tossed the CD into a box marked DEMOS behind her, where it landed on dozens of other demo CDs.

"Well?" Andrea asked, as soon as Taylor came out.

They started walking back to the car. "Well, what?"

"What did they say?"

"She thought I was cute," Taylor said. "The usual. Go away and come back when you're eighteen. Kids don't listen to country." She pouted and shrugged. "Maybe they don't *now*," she said. "But they will. *I* listen to it!" She thought about it for a moment. "Can we go back to the motel and see if anybody called?" she asked.

They both got into the car. "Sure, honey," Andrea said and started the car. When the traffic was clear, she pulled out and drove away.

Back at the motel, Taylor stared at her mom, who was on the phone with her dad back in Wyomissing. She blew him a goodbye kiss, hung up, and managed a smile in her daughter's direction.

Taylor crossed her arms. "That's not a real smile," she said.

Andrea put her arm around her daughter. "You're too smart for me," she said.

"What'd Dad say?" Taylor asked. "Who called?"

"Sorry, Tay," Andrea said.

"*No one?*" Taylor said, trying to figure out where to look. She didn't want to look into her mom's eyes because she might cry, and she didn't want to do that.

Andrea heard the disappointment in her voice. "You're not giving up, are you?"

"Heck no," Taylor said. "Maybe we should stay a few more days."

"Not a chance," Andrea said, shaking her head. "Vacation's over. You gotta get back to school. We are leaving tonight, so let's get packed," she said.

Then the phone rang.

Andrea snatched up the receiver. The man at the other end said he was an executive at a music company and he came across Taylor's demo with the real cute picture on the front. "Who am I speaking with?" he asked.

"This is Taylor's mother, Andrea Swift."

"I'd like to speak with Taylor, if I may," he continued. "I called the number on the CD and your husband gave me this number, Mrs. Swift," he said politely.

Andrea turned to her daughter and handed the phone to her. "It's for you!"

Taylor's blue eyes grew wide as she took the phone and held it to her ear. "Yes? This is Taylor Swift," she said, then paused and listened to the man talk.

Andrea couldn't hear what they were saying so she moved closer and tried to put her ear closer to the receiver.

Taylor nodded. "Uh-huh," she said and listened some more. "Okay, thank you," she said and hung up.

Andrea could not wait anymore. "Well?!" she blurted out.

"He said I was cute," Taylor said, dejected. "Don't need a weather man to tell me *that*," she said.

Andrea could see she was disappointed. "What else did he say, honey?"

"He had some advice and said it probably was worth what I paid for it, which was nothing, but he was going to say it anyway," Taylor said, pursing her lips.

"And..." Andrea said.

"And... he said everybody brings him karaoke demos of other peoples' songs. He said I had a good voice and I was cute and I would go far. But I gotta try something new instead of just singing other peoples' songs."

"How dare *he!*" Andrea protested.

Taylor hung her head, heartbroken, then went over to the bed and fell back on it and sighed.

Andrea got the family car on the road by 9:00 p.m. Taylor sat in front and Austin in back. It was a 650-mile drive from Nashville, Tennessee to Wyomissing, Pennsylvania and they were going to drive all night and all day the next day and then some to get home in one piece.

Taylor stayed up and watched the scenery roll by in the dark, just outside her window. She thought about many things, including new things she should try. "You know what I gotta do, Mom," Taylor said.

"What's that, Tay?"

"I've been thinking. Maybe that guy was right. About my CD. It's just karaoke versions of other people's songs," she said. "Ronnie said the same thing. He said I should learn to play."

"What do you want to do, honey?" Andrea asked.

"Something else. Something different." She went back to daydreaming. Wasn't she almost twelve? Didn't she already have many amazing memories about growing up? Didn't she already write hundreds of poems? And even a book? She could tell her story in songs. She thought back to how she got to Nashville in the first place. She remembered how some books by famous authors started with the line, "I am born." Although she did not remember her own birth, she knew all about it because Mom and Dad talked about it all the time, so it was a memory in her head for as long as she could remember. It all started at a Christmas tree farm, where she was born in Cumru Township, Pennsylvania. She thought back to that snow flurry Mom always talked about on that special day in December of 1989.

TWO

Andrea Swift, bathed in sweat, charged her black Quarter Horse between two endless rows of Christmas trees. There was plenty of snow on the ground and that special Christmas of 1989 was fast approaching. It was early in the morning and Pine Ridge Farm, the Swift family Christmas tree farm, would be opening in a couple of hours. It had warmed during the night and a ground fog engulfed the Pennsylvania hills like an ocean of white.

Andrea approached the farmhouse at full gallop and saw her husband Scott waiting patiently for her on the porch. She slowed her horse and trotted it up to the porch. "It's time," she said.

An hour later, they arrived at Reading Hospital in nearby West Reading, where their daughter, Taylor Alison Swift, was born the next morning at 5:17 a.m. on the fourth floor maternity ward. It was December 13, twelve days before Christmas. "I'm sorry, did you say Taylor?" the pediatric nurse asked. She held a clipboard and wanted the name of the baby for the birth certificate.

"Yes," Andrea replied. "Taylor Alison."

"Please don't think me rude, but isn't Taylor a boy's name?" the nurse asked.

"Is it?" Andrea asked.

The nurse looked from Scott to Andrea, flustered. "I suppose it could be both," she said.

"Exactly," Andrea said, giving her husband a wink. They had decided on Taylor because Andrea, a businesswoman, thought women were not treated equally in business and if their daughter was going to get a fair shot, they wanted her to a have name that would not betray her.

The nurse finished the paperwork and brought it over for Scott and Andrea to sign. She went to the bassinette and gently picked up Taylor and wrapped her in a blanket. "Welcome to the world, Taylor Alison Swift," she said and handed the baby to Andrea. The pediatrician hurried in just as the nurse was leaving. "Good morning," he said and went directly to baby Taylor. "Feeling good?" he asked as he examined Taylor.

"Elated," Andrea said.

He put out his finger and Taylor gripped it. And smiled. He was surprised. He turned to Andrea. "She's really goodnatured," he said.

"Thank you," Andrea said.

Taylor started crying and Andrea reached for her.

"But," the doctor said without missing a beat. "She knows exactly what she wants and how to get it," he said. "I'll be back tomorrow. Congratulations again. I meant what I said about..." He glanced at his clipboard. "...Taylor." Then he smiled at the new parents. "I'll see you first thing in the morning," he said as he walked out of the room.

Andrea looked to Scott. "What is he on?" she said. "He's not on anything. He just thinks Taylor is good natured," Scott said. "Of course, he left out brilliant. And beautiful." They both shared a laugh.

Four days later, Andrea and Scott Swift brought their newborn daughter home. Andrea went out ahead of them and aimed the video camera at Scott, who carried Taylor from their Wagoneer up the snow-shoveled walkway to the front door. Andrea's mother, Marjorie Finlay, who lived with them, was at the front door to welcome them. Marjorie hooked her arm in Scott's for support. "Here comes Daddy with the baby home from the hospital," Andrea said, narrating her home movie. "And her nanny," she added and Marjorie chuckled.

"They said it would never happen," Scott said. It seemed as if Andrea was pregnant forever and both of them thought Taylor would never come.

For the next few months, Taylor slept in a crib Scott had fixed up for her in the room next to their bedroom. When she awakened in the middle of the night, Grandma Marjorie tiptoed in. She rested her arm on the crib and sang very softly to Taylor. Marjorie, a former professional opera singer, had a magnificent voice. Eventually, both of them fell fast asleep. She told everyone that nothing was as satisfying to her now as singing to her granddaughter.

When Taylor was nine months old, she stood on the porch and watched her mother ride up on her Quarter Horse. She reached out her hands. "Me!" she shouted as she shook her white-blonde corkscrew curls in frustration and waved her arms around.

"I see you," Andrea said and dismounted. "All right, I guess now is as good a time as any," she said.

Taylor's eyes darted all around as she rode in front of Andrea on the black Quarter Horse, gripping the horse's mane with all her might. Her mother kept her cradled on the English saddle like a cocoon. Taylor sneezed when the mane brushed her face. She looked back at her mother and smiled broadly and Andrea knew she had done the right thing.

While Andrea guided the horse gently around the farm, Taylor watched everything. She had never seen her world from this high up and she loved it. They passed the tractor that pulled the long Christmas tree trailer from the distant fields, soon to be filled with trees in three months. They walked past the tall hedgerow that acted as a wind block from the growing fields of Christmas trees. The hedge and the surrounding trees had turned to bright shades of gold and brown and red in Taylor's first autumn. As they walked along the short stretch of grass that opened onto one of the fields growing Christmas trees, Taylor squeezed her legs tight so she would not bump along in the saddle as she rode, just like mom had taught her, and listened to the slow rhythm of the hoof beats. After a minute, she began to sing. It was not really a song; it was more of a hum. Just the same, she made it up, and more importantly, Andrea liked it. "Where'd you learn that, Tay?" she asked.

"Gramma and me," Taylor said.

THREE

Taylor, wearing her nightgown, snuggled under the covers and waited.

"Good night, sweetie," Andrea said, turning off the light.

"Hey!" Taylor shouted in the dark and Andrea turned the light back on.

"What is it?" Andrea asked.

"What about my story?" Taylor asked, pouting.

Andrea grinned. "You're right," she said and went over to the bed, pulling up a small chair. "How could I forget? You always remind me about the two things you love."

"Poems and stories," Taylor announced. Andrea looked at her daughter for a moment and the baby kicked a little and she jumped.

"What's wrong?"

"Nothing, honey. Austin just kicked, that's all." She was already overdue to deliver their second child. They knew it was a boy so they had named him a month ago.

Then she picked up the book on the bed table and opened it to the first page. "Mom, wait," Taylor said. She was looking past her mother to the closet. The door was partway open. "Please close it," she said.

Andrea studied her daughter for a moment, then went over and gently closed the closet door. "Why?" she asked, jerking her head toward the closed closet.

"There might be a monster in there," Taylor said.

Andrea pursed her lips. "Oh honey, there's no such thing as monsters."

"Are you sure?" Taylor replied.

Andrea studied her daughter for a moment.

"I guarantee you there are no monsters in that closet," she said, returned to her seat, and started reading again about all the animals on Big Bird's farm. Taylor loved this book because she lived on a farm too. Slowly, as her mother read, she closed her eyes and fell asleep.

The next day, on March 11, 1992, the Swifts had a son in the same West Reading hospital where Taylor was born. They named him Austin Kingsley Swift: Austin, after the capital of Texas, the state where Andrea was born. She was actually born in Houston, Texas, and Andrea and Scott met in Harris, Texas, but Houston was no name for a boy and Harris was too stuffy, so they named him Austin Kingsley. Austin also means *great* in Greek, and the name Kingsley was his father's middle name, which had been passed down to them from Scott's great grandmother, Barbara Maria Jane Kingsley.

The day Austin was born, Taylor sprinted into the hospital room and rushed to her mother's bedside to have a look at her new brother. "Let me see, let me see!" Taylor said, coming around the side of the bed where Austin was just waking up. She peeled away the blanket to reveal his little face.

Austin began to cry.

"Ohhhh," Taylor sighed and wrapped her arms around him, all swaddled in a new blue blanket. "This is the best day ever!" she said.

Two weeks later, on the twenty-fifth of March, 1992, two-year-old Taylor was in the family room, sitting at her little piano when the rest of the family gathered before supper. Andrea and Scott came from the kitchen. Andrea carried Austin, her newborn son.

When Marjorie came down the stairs from her room, Taylor lit up. "Gramma!" she said and ran up to her and hugged her skirt.

"Sing something, Mom," Andrea said.

Marjorie looked around the room. "Thought you'd never ask," she kidded.

"Yay!" Taylor cheered.

Marjorie sang part of Mařenka's beautiful aria from *The Bartered Bride* by nineteenth-century Czech composer, Smetana, an opera she knew every note by heart. When she finished, everyone applauded, especially Taylor.

Marjorie happily snatched up her granddaughter and sat her down at her little black piano in another part of the room. "Okay, Tay," she said. "Your turn."

Taylor was prepared. They had rehearsed this earlier. She looked around the room and waited for everyone to settle. When the room grew quiet, she took a deep breath, slammed her hands down on the keyboard of her tiny piano, and belted out "Twinkle Twinkle, Little Star." She sang loudly and her family was delighted.

Scott filmed the whole thing with his video camera.

When Taylor finished, everyone applauded. Taylor grinned broadly, stood up, and took a bow.

"Where did she learn that?" Andrea asked Marjorie. "I didn't know she knew that song."

"She didn't. I just sang it to her this morning," Marjorie shrugged. "Once. She memorized it."

Andrea looked at Scott and Scott looked at Andrea. "Now there's a girl who knows what she wants and how to get it," Andrea said, imitating the pediatrician who had said that the day Taylor was born.

FOUR

Five-year-old Taylor ran out of the movie theater ahead of her mom and dad and Austin. She was so excited she started dancing around on the sidewalk. Above her head, the marquee read Disney's *The Lion King*.

In the car on the way back to their new home in the affluent Jersey shore community of Stone Harbor, Taylor burst into song.

"I just can't wait to be kiiiiiiinnnng!" she sang loudly and perfectly. "Are those the right words?" Scott asked softly to Andrea who was sitting next to him in the front seat.

"They sound right," Andrea replied.

"Did she just memorize that song?" he asked, stunned. "I know them all, Daddy," Taylor said, then continued to sing the whole way home. Taylor was right. She sang all the songs with all the words perfectly.

The Atlantic Ocean was warm in the summer of 1995 on the Jersey shore. The multi-story summer house that the Swifts purchased in Stone Harbor was stately and white and had a magnificent view of the beach and the water from two gigantic sun porches, one on each floor, and an observation deck on the third.

Taylor loved to play at the water's edge. Scott was nearby with his video camera filming her. When a new couple arrived and laid down their blanket, Taylor rushed up to them. "Can I sing you a song?" she asked politely.

The man and the woman were surprised and amused by Taylor's boldness. "Sure," the wife said.

Taylor began to sing "I Just Can't Wait To Be King" from *The Lion King.* All the verses.

"Is that from *The Lion King?*" the husband asked.

"Yes!" Taylor said. "I saw the movie!" Then she ran off.

Scott caught the whole thing on video and smiled to the couple, then chased after Taylor who ran up to another couple and began singing.

Summer was almost over and fall was fast approaching. There would not be many more warm days and today was their last day of the summer season in Stone Harbor. Austin was in a small inflatable wading pool on the beach that Scott had filled with a couple of inches of water to keep him cool in the New Jersey heat.

Andrea watched from a walkway to make sure her infant son did not shove something into his mouth like sand or seaweed or seawater.

Five-year-old Taylor gave up singing to the beach crowd and jumped in the water and splashed around for a few minutes, then came out, trotted over to her baby brother with a small bucket full of Atlantic Ocean water and dumped it in the beach pool. Austin giggled as the water cascaded down around him and when it stopped sloshing, he stuck his face in it, came up with a mouthful, and spit it out for the camera. "Dwink!" he giggled and everyone laughed.

Summer vacation from school was over for Taylor and the 140-mile car ride back to Reading, Pennsylvania took just a little less than three hours. Taylor sat in the backseat of the family Wagoneer with her little brother, Austin. When she saw him starting to squirm, she produced her copy of *The Giving Tree* by Shel Silverstein.

"This is my new favorite," she whispered to her brother. "I love it because it is like poetry and you know how much I love poetry," she said.

Austin nodded, then closed his eyes and before she got too far into the book, she closed her eyes too and soon they were both asleep.

After a long nap, Taylor woke up. She knew she would be starting a new school in the fall. "Mom, what's the name of the school I'm going to?" she called to the front seat.

Andrea turned around and grinned. "The Wyndcroft School," she replied.

"No more uniforms?" Taylor asked.

"No, sweetie," Andrea said. "And no more nuns. Just regular teachers. And boys," she said and winked.

"Ew," Taylor said and made a face. Her old school, the Alvernia Montessori School, was run by the Bernardine Franciscan Sisters. The Wyndcroft School was an exclusive private elementary school, nineteen miles from Reading. For Taylor, it was a school with big kids and she was looking forward to being one and making new friends.

On the first day of school, Ms. Pemrick, Taylor's first grade teacher, stood at the front of the class and gave the usual orientation speech to the kids about the proud history of the school. "Anyone know when Wyndcroft was founded?"

Taylor raised her hand. She was anything but shy and she had read the history of the school and memorized it.

"Taylor?" Ms. Pemrick asked.

"1918," she said.

"That's correct," Ms. Pemrick said. "Do you know why that year is important? Especially for us girls?"

Taylor was thrilled she was actually talking with the teacher. She shook her head. She had no idea why 1918 was important.

"It was the year women got the right to vote in America," the teacher said, then turned and started writing new spelling words on the blackboard.

Over the next year, Taylor flourished in school. Besides the books they read in class, she devoured many books at home. As a young girl heading toward second grade, her vocabulary grew and she figured out how the authors created and constructed the stories she loved to read. When Ms. Pemrick asked her students what their favorite things were, Taylor's hand shot up first.

"Poems," she said.

Taylor could see that Ms. Pemrick was intrigued. "Tell us why," the teacher said.

Taylor gnawed on her lip while she thought about it for a moment. "Because they say the exact right thing at the exact right time."

"Excellent description," her teacher said. "Do you write them yourself?"

Taylor grinned and nodded. "I handwrite them. I make them up, wherever I am. Even here," she said.

FIVE

Taylor tore the bow and the ribbon off, then ripped the wrapping off her birthday present. It was December 13, 1996 and Taylor had turned seven years old. The present was a CD of an album: LeAnn Rimes' *Blue,* released the previous summer at the start of July. It had immediately shot up to number one on the country music charts. When she unwrapped the present near the tree, Scott stood by the CD player, ready to put it on. Instead, Taylor turned it over and read the liner notes. After a few moments, she shouted, "Oh my goodness! She's only thirteen years old!"

"Bring it here, Tay, and I'll play it for you," Scott said.

Taylor did not budge from where she was sitting and continued to read the liner notes, ignoring everyone around her.

Scott shrugged. "Okay, you know how to work the CD player," he said and went into the kitchen.

Taylor just stared at the notes and kept reading. She turned the CD over and stared at LeAnn Rimes' picture on the cover. She had long, reddish-blonde hair and wore a brown lace maxi dress. She sat on the bottom stair of a ladder going up to a loft. Everything was wood. Taylor knew immediately she was in a barn. She raced out of the house and down the frozen path to the barn with the big red door. There were drifts of dirty snow everywhere. She threw open the barn door and a couple of their feral cats scattered in two directions. One of them had a field mouse in its mouth. She charged across the hay-strewn floor to the wooden ladder, just like in the LeAnn Rimes album cover, and climbed up into the loft, taking the steps two at a time. When she reached the top, she flopped out on a pile of hay she had made into a bed. This was her private place. She had placed a few milk crates around the loft and each had some of her things on them, like small tables. There was even a lamp. The hay made a perfect bed and Taylor stretched out on her back in it, held the CD cover in front of her, and read it again.

And again.

She counted on her fingers. "Seven. In six years, *I'll* be thirteen."

Scott Swift stood next to one of the Christmas trees he grew himself. It was about his height, a little over six feet tall. Taylor sat opposite him on a large rock.

"Okay," Scott said, running his gloved hand through the branches of the pine. "What we are looking for are egg cases."

Taylor knew about the egg cases. Looking for praying mantis egg cases had been her job ever since she helped her mom and dad last Christmas. She was just too short back then and couldn't reach the top branches. Now she was a lot taller than kids her age and she was old enough, just seven, to use the three-step ladder to reach the top of the trees.

"We can't let any trees leave the farm with any egg cases on them," Scott continued. "It would be terrible for business."

"But Daddy, we like the praying mantises," she said.

"That's right, we need the praying mantises because they eat all the other insects that try to infect the trees. It's like having our own free bug control. But praying mantises lay eggs in cases and they are hard to see and if a tree leaves here with any cases on it, chances are they will hatch in peoples' homes. And each case holds 300 eggs! That might be trouble!"

Taylor giggled at the thought of thousands of praying mantises hatching under the tree on Christmas morning and swarming the presents looking for other bugs to eat.

"Okay, you know what to do," her father said. "Zero eggs."

"Exactly!"

A week later, Taylor daydreamed out the dining room window. Then she glanced over to where her father was loading a Christmas tree on a customer's blue station wagon. Her eyes grew wide and she stood up suddenly, shoving her chair back from the dining room table, making a loud screeching noise.

Without a word, she rushed out of the house and ran all the way to her father's side just as the station wagon pulled out of the dirt driveway and headed down the road in front of Pine Ridge Farm. Scott smiled at his daughter. "Another happy customer," he said.

"I… I hope so," Taylor said, visibly shaken.

"What do you mean?" Scott noticed something wasn't right. "What's wrong, sweetie?" he asked. "I… I forgot," she said, biting her lip.

"Forgot what?" he asked.

"I forgot to check the tree," she said, tears welling up in her eyes. "For egg cases."

Scott realized what she had just said and glanced back at the road. The car was almost out of sight. "I'm sure it will be fine," he said, unsure, and then watched as the station wagon disappeared around the distant corner that led back to town. Taylor noticed he had a worried look on his face.

"I'm sure too, Daddy," she said, also unsure. She turned away and walked back to the house with a sinking feeling in her stomach.

The man returned the next day. He had a large pickle jar full of squirming newborn mantises. "These were all I could catch," he said. "The rest got away."

"I'm so sorry!" she said and rushed away without warning. She stopped before she got to the house and turned back. "Thank you for not killing them!" Then she stormed into the house.

Later, Andrea realized her daughter was upset and sat down on the side of the bed. She waited for a few moments to see whether Taylor would start talking and when she did not, Andrea began talking. "Sooo," she said, real sing-songy. "What are you doing?"

Taylor, under the covers, could only sob. Finally, she took a deep breath, gathered her courage, and spoke.

"I'm grounded," she said.

Andrea did not even know she knew the word. "What do you mean, 'grounded'?" she asked.

"I'm just grounded," Taylor replied and shrugged.

Andrea sighed and studied the lump under the covers that was her daughter. "Relax, Tay. I'm not going to punish you for that," she said.

"I know," Taylor said and did not move. "But I am," she said.

That's Taylor all right, Andrea thought. *She is always her own toughest critic.*

She told her daughter that everyone makes mistakes, Mom and Dad included, and that she needed to move on. They needed her help with the trees.

An hour later, Taylor was back outside looking for mantises.

SIX

One night, during dinner, the doorbell rang. "I'll get it," Andrea said, pushing back from the table. "Hello, Ms. Pemrick!" Taylor heard her mother say from the front door.

Taylor's eyes grew wide. "I'm so sorry. I hope I'm not disturbing you," Taylor heard her teacher, Ms. Pemrick, say.

"Of course not, come in. Can I get you some coffee?" Taylor heard her mom say. Ms. Pemrick answered, "Oh that would be nice," and then their footsteps came into the dining room.

When Taylor saw her teacher come into the room, she did not know what to do. She had never seen Ms. Pemrick anywhere but in school.

"I won't be long," Ms. Pemrick said as Andrea brought her a steaming cup of coffee. She sipped it, then set it down. "Your daughter wrote a four-page essay today in class," she said.

"That's great!" Andrea said.

Ms. Pemrick agreed. "I had asked for one paragraph, Mrs. Swift, but Taylor wrote four pages. Both sides."

Andrea's eyes widened and she looked to her husband, slightly confused. "Okay, so you're not here because there is a problem with Taylor?"

"Oh, Lord no. Look. Usually," the teacher said, taking another sip of coffee, "if I can get a student to put four or five sentences together, I feel downright triumphant."

"I'm sorry, Ms. Pemrick," Taylor said. "I won't do it again."

Ms. Pemrick burst out laughing and Taylor joined in, unsure of what was funny. She had never really heard her laugh and she liked it. It was loud and sincere.

"What I am getting at," Ms. Pemrick said. "Is that we feel this is something that Taylor loves to do. It is so rare that a child is interested in writing that I wanted to stop by on my way home from school to urge you to nurture this in her. Honestly, she loves it!" She stood up. "Thank you for the coffee," she said. "Don't get up. I didn't mean to interrupt your supper. I just had to let you know. I'll let myself out." She walked toward the front door then turned back. "Frankly, we're thrilled," she said with a smile, then left.

When the teacher was gone, Andrea turned to her family. "Well!" she said. "That was refreshing! How about that?"

"What did you write about?" Scott asked his daughter.

"My first day in school," Taylor said. "And if I had time, I would have written more."

She saw her parents look at each other and smile.

"We're so proud of you," Andrea said.

It was Taylor's first day in second grade.

The following week, Andrea waited for her daughter to come out of school and when she saw her, it made her happy. Taylor ran to the car, skipping the whole way. She only skipped when she was happy. Andrea opened the backdoor. "What are *you* so happy about? Because it's Friday?"

"Is it?" Taylor asked and yanked the door closed behind her. Once in the car, she unzipped her parka and let out a breath of steam, which made a fleeting cloud in the car. "Look!" she said pointing at the marquee out in front of the school. Andrea looked over at it and saw that it announced the annual school Christmas play. "Are you talking about the Christmas play?"

"Yeah!" Taylor shouted, she was so excited. "Do you want to go see it?"

"No! I want to be in it!" Taylor replied.

Taylor tried out for the Wyndcroft Christmas play and landed a role as a singing toy doll. Ms. Kolvek, the music teacher, painted her cheeks rosy red and drew long eyelashes on her face. Her hair was just right: long and curly and white-blonde, tied back with a wide white ribbon, perfect for playing the part.

Taylor knew her cue to sing. The boys who were playing the toy soldiers would march around, then surround the toys and, they would all start singing the song. It was the last scene of the play. Every time she moved on stage she looked out into the audience, but she couldn't see anyone because the lights were pointing at the stage. The audience members were all just bobbing blobs in the dark.

The moment was coming and she took in a deep breath. The soldiers made their move on the stage and she sang "Jingle Bells" as loudly as she could. "Dashing through the snow, in a one-horse open sleigh! O'er the fields we go, laughing all the way! HA HA HA!" they all sang together.

Andrea and Scott and Austin watched proudly as she danced around the stage and sang with all her heart, surrounded by the toy soldiers played by her fellow students. Scott stood up and filmed her with his ever-present video camera. Taylor had a beautiful voice and they could hear her above all the rest of the players on stage.

When the song was over, the lights came up and all the children on stage joined hands and bowed. The play was over. The audience roared, cheering wildly with unbridled applause. Taylor felt the sounds of the audience's delight against her chest, in waves of energy. She felt it all and it felt like love. During the melee she found her family in the audience, cheering and clapping. She closed her eyes and let the applause flow over her and through her. She remembered the praise she got when she sang for her mom and dad and for the people on the beach, during the summers when she would sing songs from her favorite Disney movies. This time it was different. It was unlike anything she had ever felt before and she instantly knew one thing for sure: she wanted more.

SEVEN

On Christmas the following year, Taylor had just turned eight, and everything changed for her when she unwrapped the one special Christmas present from Santa Claus. Of course, as in all things that unfold in a child's life, no one knew at the time the significance of the present. It was an acoustic guitar. A nice one, with simple ivory inlays down the cherry wood fingerboard. The tuners were top of the line.

She showed it around to her folks and brother and grandma, who were all gathered around the Christmas tree. "Look!" she said. "It has my name on it!" There it was in bold flowery letters, the name *TAYLOR* inlayed on a piece of ebony. It would be a while before she realized that the name was not custom-inlayed for her but was, rather, the brand of guitar.

For her birthday earlier in the month, she had gotten a bunch of girly-girl stuff, some clothes, some makeup to play with, a new riding helmet covered in navy blue cloth with blue, yellow, and magenta triangles all over it. But for Christmas, she got the guitar. It was awesome. Now she could be a country star just like LeAnn Rimes. She pointed the guitar neck to the left and strummed the strings with her right fingers. It sounded terrible and out of tune and she winced. She tried to put her fingers on the neck, bent into weird positions like how Dolly and LeAnn did it, to form a chord, but her hands were too small and her fingers were too short and she could not press down hard enough on the steel strings to make the right sounds. She wiggled her fingers. "They won't fit!" she said, frustrated.

"Don't worry, Tay," Scott said. "You'll grow into it." Taylor thought about it for a moment, then said, "Okay, Daddy." Her father always knew the right thing to say. She had instantly fallen in love with the instrument even though she could not play it. After the presents were open, Taylor took her new guitar to her room and placed it in a corner so she could always see it and dream about playing it someday.

Later that night, she read the small manual that came with the guitar. It basically showed how to play a few rudimentary chords, which were too difficult for her tiny fingers. After she read the manual, cover to cover, she left it on a shelf near the guitar and went over to her bed and flopped out on it. Lying there, she glanced over at her nightstand where she kept the pad of lined paper she wrote her poems in. She kept it with her favorite books, *The Giving Tree* by Shel Silverstein and various books by Dr. Seuss. She loved the way Dr.

Seuss wrote poetry. When he didn't have a word that rhymed, he made one up. She understood the power of words because *The Giving Tree* always made her cry. It was her favorite story. It was about a female tree and a boy who grow up together. She asked her mom how it was possible to make words up and make people feel with words and Andrea said it was because English was a very flexible language. You could bend it every which way and get people to laugh and cry and feel.

She glanced across the room and sure enough, her closet door was slightly open. She opened the notebook and thumbed past poem after poem she had written on the pages in pencil and ink and kept thumbing until she found a new blank page. She picked up her pen that she kept always within reach and began to write:

"There's a monster in my closet and I don't know what to do!"

She heard her mom's footsteps on the stairs coming up to her room and spirited the book away under her pillow. A moment later, Andrea peeked her head into the room and saw the light on above her daughter's bed. "No more writing tonight, Tay-Tay," she said. "Light's out."

"Yes, Mom," Taylor said and turned out the light, bathing the room in darkness except for a chevron of moonlight streaming in from the window.

"Merry Christmas," Andrea said, then closed the door.

As soon as the door closed, Taylor listened for a moment, then when she heard no sounds out in the hall, turned the light back on.

Out in the hall, Andrea stood by Taylor's bedroom door and saw the sliver of light go on under the door and grinned. She knew what it was like to have a passion. It was what drove her into the marketing business years ago. It was what drove her to succeed. And she knew her daughter had a passion too. She took one last look at the light under the door, then walked away.

After her mom shut the door, Taylor began flipping through her book of poems where she had written about the monster in her closet. She added a line under the first line:

"Have you ever seen him? Has he ever pounced on you?"

She smiled to herself and put her pencil down. It was a poem unlike any other poem she had written. It was as different as *The Giving Tree* was a different kind of book. She placed the notebook back on her nightstand, took one last look at her copy of *The Giving Tree,* then flicked off the light.

When Taylor was eight, winter gave way to spring and spring to summer. And for Taylor, Wyomissing gave way to the Jersey shore. The Swift beach house in Stone Harbor was large and white and had an ocean view. Taylor stared at herself in the mirror in her bedroom and drew a mark on the right side of the indent above her top lip. She stretched the skin a bit and twisted the dark brown eyebrow pencil, creating a perfectly fake beauty mark.

Austin looked up from his Legos with less than zero interest, made a face, and went back to playing. He had no idea what she was doing.

Taylor's heart raced. Tonight was the concert, her first, and she just didn't think going plain-faced was good enough. After she finished at the mirror, she gathered up some of her poems and copied them onto art paper. She wrote notes on other blank pages. Then when she had enough pages, she folded them, drew on the cover, and used her dad's duct tape to put the whole thing together into a book. She was ready: the book was done and her beauty mark was just right. After all, this was her first concert and everything had to be perfect.

The casino where LeAnn Rimes was playing was 27 miles from Stone Harbor. Scott drove up the Garden State Parkway and made good time, considering the weekend traffic. He knew how important this concert was to Taylor and he had managed to get them all front row seats. Taylor could barely sit down. "Please talk to them, Daddy!" she said, waving the handmade book around. Scott finally got up and went to a security guard standing at one side of the stage and spoke to him for a minute. The guard nodded and went away and when he returned he brought a woman with him who was wearing a big backstage pass around her neck that said *LeAnn Rimes VIP*.

Scott looked at Taylor and waved her over and Taylor raced to him, almost tripping along the way.

"Hi Taylor," the lady said. "I hear you have something for LeAnn."

Taylor just stared for a moment, unable to find the words. Finally, she shoved the handmade book at her. "Here! This is for LeAnn! I love her!" she said.

The woman took the book. "I'll make sure she gets it," she said, gave Taylor a big hug, then hurried backstage.

Taylor couldn't believe it. She walked back to her seat. "Thank you, Daddy," she said and took her seat.

An hour later, in the middle of the concert, between songs, LeAnn stepped close to the mic and amid the thundering applause and cheering, said, "Thanks for the book, Taylor!"

Taylor screamed and leaped to her feet. "She knows my name!" she shouted and reached her hand out. When LeAnn saw her, she trotted over and touched her hand. "I'm going to keep it forever," she said privately to her, then trotted back and the band resumed and she went on to the next song.

On the drive back to the Jersey shore, after the concert, Taylor protected her hand as if it were made of gold.

Scott glanced in his rearview mirror. "Something wrong with that hand?"

"I'm never going to wash it, 'cuz LeAnn touched it," Taylor said and they all laughed.

EIGHT

Taylor sat in the auditorium seat in the first row, transfixed, looking up at her music teacher, Barbara Kolvek. Ms. Kolvek was on the stage pacing back and forth, explaining this year's school Christmas play. It was going to be *The Runaway Snowman* by Jill Gallina.

"There will be eight songs in this great play, all rock style, and all arranged to be sung in unison so that everyone gets a chance to sing," the teacher said.

Taylor's hand shot up.

Ms. Kolvek tried to continue, but Taylor's hand kept waving more and more wildly in the audience. She finally stopped talking and called on her. "Yes, Taylor?"

"I looked at the libretto and there are actually seven songs that are sung in unison. One of them is a solo."

"You're right, Taylor," Ms. Kolvek said. "'I Want To Make You A Star' is sung solo. Thank you for doing your homework on this."

Taylor beamed proudly.

"I assume you are interested in playing the part of Robin, the female lead?"

"No ma'am. I want to sing the solo—"I Want to Make You a Star!"

Ms. Kolvek looked confused. "But that's sung by Freddy Fasttalk, the bad guy."

"That's right!" Taylor replied. "I want to play Freddy Fasttalk!"

"But Taylor, Freddy Fasttalk is a man," the teacher said.

Taylor shrugged. "Yes. He has bushy eyebrows and a moustache. Just put them on me. I don't care what I look like, I just want to sing that song!" Taylor said.

The students in the auditorium laughed and Taylor laughed with them.

But she got what she wanted.

The first time Taylor strode out on the stage as Freddy Fasttalk, she owned it. She wore blue farmer overalls, a blue baseball cap, exaggerated cartoon eyebrows, and a thick cartoonish moustache that made her look like one of the Super Mario brothers. She thought up the costume herself. She sang her heart out and the audience loved her.

Andrea, Scott, and Austin were in the audience and when Taylor came out for a bow, they stood up and clapped the loudest. "Was she singing in a Southern accent?" Scott whispered to Andrea as Taylor bowed.

Andrea nodded. "Just a little bit. It's all that country music she listens to," she whispered back.

Scott chuckled, then returned his attention to the stage as Taylor and the cast took another bow. The audience kept on cheering. And Taylor loved every minute of it.

Later that year, when Taylor was almost ten, she rode her Quarter Horse fast, almost creating a whirlwind behind them as they galloped down the long row of Christmas trees toward the snow-covered Pine Ridge farmhouse. She arced her horse with precision over the watercourse without ever leaving the saddle. She had already won several awards for riding on exciting courses, but the Pine Ridge thoroughfare was still her favorite, because it was difficult and it was real. Being able to practice on it every day gave her the edge.

When she got to the horse barn, her mom was there trimming flowers.

"Did it come?!" Taylor shouted, breathless from her morning ride.

"On the table," Andrea said, not looking up.

Taylor swung her long leg over the horn, slid to the ground without missing a beat, and ran into the house. Her horse walked the few steps over to Andrea and nudged her, almost knocking her over. She laughed.

Taylor tore into the dining room and scattered the day's mail all over the long table, searching for it, finally finding the package. It was addressed to her. From Grandma. She ripped it open. It was the new CD by The Dixie Chicks, *Wide Open Spaces,* that had just come out a few days earlier. It was their fourth album and the first album with their new lead, Natalie Maines. Taylor put her headphones on and listened to the entire album nonstop. When the last cut played, she fought the tears she rarely shed, she was so blown away. "Oh... my... God!" she shouted at the ceiling, louder than she ever had before.

Andrea rushed to the doorway. "What's wrong?!"

Taylor looked over at her mom and pulled off one of her headphones. "Best album *ever!*"

Andrea shook her head and rolled her eyes and started to walk away.

"Mom?" Taylor called after her.

Andrea stopped and peeked her head back in the room. "Yes...?"

"This settles it! I love country music!" Taylor said.

A few months later, Scott Swift bought a mansion in Wyomissing Hills, closer to Taylor's school, and moved his family away from the Christmas tree farm. The new home had three stories and an indoor swimming pool. Taylor got the third floor all to herself.

Taylor stood in the doorway, holding her guitar, and looked at her room, frozen in place. Her mom came up behind her and put her hands on her daughter's shoulders. "All for you, Tay," she said. "You can play your music as loud as you want."

Taylor held back her tears. It was like a dream come true.

NINE

The new house on Grandview was grand indeed. It was a three-story, red brick classical revival with a steeply pitched roof and three belvederes on it facing the road, a window in each one. Moving to the big house in Wyomissing Hills was the reward for Scott Swift's hard work and his growing family. The neighborhood was as good as it gets and the mansion had a spectacular view of the surrounding Pennsylvania countryside in all directions.

And the home was close to West Reading Elementary School, Taylor's new school.

West Reading Elementary School was on Chestnut Street, a ten-minute drive from the new house. The most prominent building was two-story and made all of red brick, with a basement. Taylor's fifth-grade teacher was Mrs. Boyer, who wore nice clothes and no makeup. She had blue eyes and medium-cropped red hair. A few weeks into the semester, during the section of the day she dedicated to Language Arts, Mrs. Boyer wrote the words *Creative Communication Poetry Contest.*

When she finished, she smashed a period at the end of the sentence hard on the blackboard with her stick of chalk. She turned back to the class and brushed the chalk dust off her hands. "Creative Communication is a company in Utah. They hold a contest every year for fifth and sixth graders," she said. "They pick the top ten poems from all over the country in each grade and publish them in a big book of poems. Who can define a poem?"

Taylor's hand shot up.

"Taylor?"

She knew what it was. After all, she had already written a whole book full of them. "A poem is the perfect combination of words, with the perfect amount of syllables and the perfect rhyme that makes it pop off the page," she said without hesitation.

The class grew pin-drop silent. The students were surprised at her answer and Taylor was surprised at their silence. Did they not understand? She was not sure.

Mrs. Boyer was amazed. "Um," she said, searching for the words. She had not expected such a perceptive response. "Y-yes, I suppose that is a good definition of a poem," she said. "I've just not heard it put that way."

"How would *you* put it, Mrs. Boyer?" Taylor asked.

"Well," Mrs. Boyer said, gathering her thoughts.

"The dictionary defines it as a 'piece of writing that expresses emotions, experiences, and ideas,'" she said, then could not remember the rest so she snatched up her dictionary and opened it to the right page.

"'Especially in short lines using words that rhyme,'" she continued to read, finishing the book definition. She looked up and snapped her book shut. "I like your definition better," she said.

Taylor flashed a smile.

"In fact, it was absolutely refreshing." Taylor's heart raced. "Thank you," she said.

"I take it you are interested in entering the contest?" Taylor grinned. "Yes!" She knew which poem she wanted to submit the moment Mrs. Boyer announced the contest. "I think I have the perfect poem for it."

Some kids in the class groaned. They thought she was stuck up.

The next morning Taylor was already at the kitchen table eating a bowl of cereal when her mother and father came down for breakfast. "Good morning!" she said.

Her greeting cheered them up.

"I was thinking I would go with the gimmicky one," she said and continued eating.

Scott sat down at the table. "Are we supposed to know what you are talking about?" he asked.

"The poetry contest, Mr. Swift," Andrea said, starting the coffee. "Get with the program."

"I don't want to go too dark on them," Taylor said.

"You don't want to go too dark on *who*?" Scott asked.

"On the poetry contest judges, silly!" Taylor said. "I have a lot of gloomy stuff, but this one is fun. I think they'll like it."

Taylor had her book of poems on the table and she opened it to a bookmarked page. "It took me forever to get the perfect combination of words with just the right amount of syllables," she said, finding the poem she was going to enter into the contest.

An hour later, Mrs. Boyer stood in the front of the class, taking roll. When she was finished, she put the attendance book down on her desk and turned back to the class. "Who brought in a poem to enter the contest?"

She looked around the room. No one raised their hand.

Taylor was on her own. She periscoped her hand up slowly.

"Taylor?" Mrs. Boyer said with a big smile. "Would you please come up and read it to us?"

"Yes, ma'am," Taylor said and walked up the aisle to the front, amid some groans from the boys.

TEN

Taylor sat outside the classroom reading *To Kill A Mockingbird* by Harper Lee for the second time, waiting for class to start. Her teacher, Mrs. Boyer, hurried by and took the stairs two at a time, stepping around Taylor as she got to the doorway of her classroom. "Got a surprise for you, Taylor," she said and went inside.

The classroom was empty except for Mrs. Boyer because it was still a few minutes too early for the students to arrive. Taylor always came early.

Mrs. Boyer held an envelope from Creative Communication in Logan, Utah. The poetry contest people. It had been just about a month since she submitted Taylor's poem. It was a funny little poem about a monster in her closet, Taylor had explained to the class. She said that it was based on her life. She had explained to Mrs. Boyer why she thought this would be the best poem for her to submit: because it was different than what the contest runners would be expecting. It would be unique and that's how you stand out, Taylor told her. Mrs. Boyer had never had a fifth-grader like Taylor before.

When class started, Mrs. Boyer stood up front and fanned the letter in front of the class as if it was the envelope announcing the winner of an Academy Award. "I have a letter here," Mrs. Boyer said. "A letter from Creative Communication in Logan, Utah."

No one in the class reacted. They had no idea what she was talking about because no one in the class had bothered to submit a poem of their own. No one but Taylor Alison Swift.

"Taylor?" Mrs. Boyer continued. "Would you please step up here?"

Taylor felt like her chest was going to explode, her heart was beating so fast. Despite a few groans from some of the students, and the usual rolling of the eyes, Taylor charged up to the front of the class. She wanted to walk calmly, like a lady, but her legs were long and she was so excited, she could not help herself.

"Taylor, I want to congratulate you. You've won the national Creative Communication annual poetry contest for the fifth grade! For your poem "Monster in My Closet!"

There was a long loud silent pause in the classroom and Taylor's heart sunk. Were the other students going to hate her for this? She did not have to wait long because, a moment later, the entire class cheered her and applauded her.

Mrs. Boyer handed her the letter, while she addressed the class. "Your poem is being published in their annual anthology of poetry! Congratulations, Taylor Swift! You are officially a published poet!"

Taylor stood in front of the class in disbelief, her knees knocking because she was so nervous, as her fellow students cheered her on. Even the boys! She fought back the tears. She was a poet! The kids had never reacted this way before. On her way back to her seat, one of the boys even put his hand up and she high-fived him. "Real cool, Tay," he said.

Taylor blushed. And sat down quickly. She had never really thought about boys before except as creatures that poked fun at her and were generally a nuisance. No boy had ever complimented her before except her father.

A few weeks later, Andrea dropped a stack of *The Reading Eagle* newspapers on the kitchen table. "I bought every copy they had," she said to Taylor who was already at the table munching an after-school snack.

"Oh boy!" Taylor said and snatched up a copy of the paper. There on the front page was a short article on her winning the poetry contest. The headline said it all: "Two Berks Pupils Honored in Statewide Poetry Contest." There was a picture of her with her hair in cornrows and a picture of the other person who won for Pennsylvania.

Taylor devoured the article, then something else on the page caught her eye. She read something else. "Amazing!"

"Yes, you are, honey," Andrea agreed.

"No, not me," Taylor said. "Look!" She pointed to a banner advertisement on the same page.

Andrea gazed over and saw the banner ad for the Berks County Youth Theatre Academy and read it.

The theatre group was holding open auditions for their next play, *Annie*. She looked up and Taylor was watching her anxiously.

"What do you think?" Taylor asked. "They put on three plays a year!"

Andrea was still confused. "What do you want, Tay?" "I want to audition!" Taylor exclaimed again. "Please take me!"

Andrea looked at her daughter with wonder. "You are just like your grandmother," she said. "Do you really want to get up on stage in front of all those strangers and act and sing?"

"More than anything," Taylor replied.

The Berks County Youth Theatre Academy was in the nearby township of Temple, Pennsylvania on Kutztown Road. It was a two-story flagstone building with a basement and attic windows facing the street, double doors, and awnings over the windows. When Taylor went in through the front doors, the auditions were already in progress. Andrea hung in the back and Taylor found an empty seat next to a tall girl named

Kaylin Politzer. They started talking immediately and discovered they went to the same school. Kaylin pointed out her mother in the back of the room and when Taylor turned around to look, she saw her mother talking with Kaylin's mom.

"Look at that, the two tall girls found each other," a mother said who stood next to Andrea in the back of the room. She introduced herself as Mrs. Politzer. "Kaylin's mom," she said.

"Kaylin?" Andrea asked.

"The girl your daughter is sitting next to. She *is* your daughter, right? I saw you come in with her. She's very pretty, by the way," Mrs. Politzer said. "Can she sing?"

"Like a bird," Andrea said proudly. "Have you done this before?"

"Kay's been in BYTA for about a year," she said.

"Bite-a?" Andrea asked.

"That's what we call it here. B-Y-T-A. Berks County Youth Theatre Academy. Long name, so we gave it a shortcut so we would have some air left after we said it."

Andrea chuckled. She liked her. "Any advice?"

Mrs. Politzer looked up as the director, Kirk Cremer, called Kaylin's name and Kaylin stood and went through an open door to the room beyond. Cremer was in his late twenties with thinning hair and a polished smile. Mrs. Politzer turned to Andrea. "Impress *him*," she said indicating Kirk Cremer. "Who's that?" Andrea asked.

"The director."

ELEVEN

Taylor waited anxiously to be called in for her audition. Kaylin's name was called and Kaylin went through a doorway. She knew the people who decided who would be in the play and who wouldn't be were behind that door and she grew nervous. She had never really auditioned for a play before, other than the Christmas plays she did in elementary school. This was professional.

The door looked like the closet door in all her rooms, open just a little bit.

Moments later, Kaylin came out, traipsed back to her seat, and plunked down next to Taylor. "Whew. Glad that's over."

Taylor's hands shook and she sat on them.

Kaylin looked at Taylor's hidden hands, then up to her eyes. "You and I are outsiders," she said softly.

"Shhh," Taylor said as politely as possible. "Not so loud," she whispered.

"Don't worry, it's okay to talk. I've been here about a year. This is my fourth play."

"So you got in?" Taylor asked.

Kaylin just smiled.

Taylor managed a tight-lipped smile, but she was definitely nervous. She knew that meant she must really want this.

"This play has a big cast, so no worries. We're all going to get a part. If *I* can get one, anyone can get one."

"Taylor Swift," the voice said and the door opened. It was Kirk Cremer.

Taylor stood up.

"That would be you," Kaylin said and took her hand. "Outsiders, remember that."

"*Why* do you think we are outsiders?" Taylor whispered.

"Tall? Awkward? We're here instead of watching reality shows," Kaylin replied. "We're here 'cuz we're not all there."

Taylor laughed. She liked Kaylin. She was funny. She looked at the door that was left open for her and calmed down. She walked up the aisle and passed through the open door. A moment later, it closed behind her.

Kaylin got the role of Pepper, one of Little Orphan Annie's friends, and Taylor was cast as an "extra orphan," another one of Annie's friends. She read for the part facing a table with three people sitting at it:

Kirk Cremer, the director, and his assistants at the theatre academy. When she finished singing, everyone at the table applauded. "You have a beautiful voice, Taylor. I want to work with you," the director told her. "I'm not just a director, I'm also a voice coach."

"Voice coach? You can help my singing?" Taylor asked.

"I can help that Southern twang, yes," he replied. "The orphans in this play are from the streets of New York, not the suburbs of Nashville."

Taylor blushed. "Sorry, sir, I listen to a lot of LeAnn Rimes and Dixie Chicks," the ten-year-old told him. "I guess it rubbed off."

Kirk laughed. "Don't worry," he replied. "I'll fix it."

Taylor smiled back and looked him in the eye. "I'm not worried." She took a moment to let that register, then thanked him and left. Once her back was to them, she grinned broadly. She had made it. When she came into the waiting room, she shot Kaylin two thumbs up.

When Taylor took the stage for the first time, playing an "extra orphan," she was taller than the rest of the girls and Kirk Cremer could not take his eyes off her. She commanded the stage and did a fantastic job. Her voice cut through the rest. He had not expected that from the new girl in town.

After the month-long run of performances, BYTA had a wrap party, which included food, drinks, friends, and a karaoke machine. Taylor and Kaylin came together, along with Scott and Andrea Swift. The girls danced together for the first part of the night, until "There's Your Trouble" by the Dixie Chicks came up on the machine and no one went for the mic.

Taylor saw the song come up out of the corner of her eye and could not resist. "Be right back," she said to Kaylin and hurried over to the stage.

Kaylin's eyes went wide when she saw her best friend go up front and grab the microphone just as the music began. "This is a song from the Dixie Chicks' album, *Wide Open Spaces,* called 'There's Your Trouble,'" she said into the mic, introducing the song. Then she came into the music perfectly and belted out the song.

Kirk Cremer stood in the middle of the dance floor and stopped dancing when he heard Taylor sing the song perfectly. An older woman stepped up to Kirk and whispered in his ear, "Did you know about this?"

It was Kirk's mother. Her name was Sandy Wieder, and she worked in the entertainment field, booking and representing acts.

"Know about what, Mom?" Kirk asked. "That she could sing country?"

"Yeah," he replied, never taking his eyes off Taylor as she sang.

All the guests at the party stopped what they were doing and listened to her sing.

"I've been trying to get rid of that Southern accent of hers for months."

"For God's sake, stop," Sandy said. "She's a natural." She moved on, leaving Kirk to think about it.

A few months later, Taylor stood in line at the familiar table and waited her turn to sign up to audition for a part in BYTA's next play, *The Sound of Music*. When it was her turn, Taylor stepped up to Kirk Cremer and his staff at the table, this time unafraid.

Kirk looked up and smiled when he saw it was Taylor. "Welcome back, Tay. What role are you reading for?"

"I don't need to read, Mr. Cremer. I just want to be in the chorus again," she said. "Or one of the kids, you know."

Kirk smiled politely. "I don't think so," he replied.

Taylor was shocked. "But I thought you *liked* me in *Annie*…" For a second she thought even though everyone had told her that she had done a great job, they were really lying and that she actually was really bad.

"You did a great job in *Annie*," Kirk replied, handing her a set of sides for *The Sound of Music*. Sides were only pages of a given role, separated out so the actor or actress could learn the lines. "That's why I want you to read for the role of Maria," he said.

Taylor stood stock still for an eternity, not exactly getting what he had just said to her. "M-Maria?!" Taylor was shocked. "But… but… Maria is the *lead!*"

Kirk smiled. "That's right, Tay," he said. "I want you to read for the lead."

TWELVE

Taylor read for the part of Maria, just like Kirk Cremer had asked, and did such a spectacular job, he cast her on the spot. Seeing the rest of the girls who went out for the part was just a formality in his mind. He believed Taylor was made for the part: she was tall and commanded the stage whenever she took it. He could see her in the play as no one else.

Her voice was polished and could hit all the ranges required of Maria's role. And it was almost as if Taylor's life coincided with the life of Maria, a woman who sought peace with the church and wound up discovering a love for music and true love in the process. Taylor completely related to the role and nailed it when it came time to audition.

A few weeks after landing the part, ten-year-old Taylor played Shania Twain full-blast on the stereo in her room. After all, her mother did tell her she could play her music as loud as she wanted. Her best friend, Kaylin, was with her and they had closed all the doors, including the closet. Kaylin sat at the table with the playbook of *The Sound of Music* and a BYTA flyer advertising it as their next play.

Taylor stood near the stereo watching Kaylin's face as they both listened. "Now that's *country!*" she shouted over the music. "Don't you think?"

Kaylin did not respond. She was distracted by something she just read on the flyer on the table in front of her. She sucked in a breath and stabbed her finger at it. "Oh my God! The play opens on Friday the thirteenth!" Kaylin said. She got up and paced around the table. "Isn't that unlucky?!"

"Says who?" "Everybody!"

"Not me," Taylor replied.

Kaylin looked at her, incredulous. "Aren't you worried?" she asked.

Taylor laughed. "Why should I be? Thirteen is my lucky number," she replied. "Our play opening on Friday the thirteenth proves it!"

Kaylin managed a smile. "Okay, you win. Let's go over our parts again." She plopped down on the bed next to Taylor as they listened to Faith Hill on the stereo.

Two weeks later, Taylor was center stage in Maria's wardrobe taking a solo bow for her performance in *The Sound of Music*. The audience was on their feet, applauding. She had made it through the first performance and did a great job.

Maria's character awakened a passion for music in the Von Trapp children and in turn awakened a passion for it in Taylor. Her grandma was in the audience and their eyes met. It was her grandma, Marjorie, the opera singer, who awakened a passion in music for her. For Taylor, it made the performance real and it showed when she left the stage.

Kirk Cremer was waiting for her with open arms. "You were brilliant!"

"Thank you!" Taylor shouted back.

He hugged her then handed her a bouquet of long-stemmed roses.

Kaylin was there and hugged her too. "You were awesome!"

Taylor hugged her back.

"Remember I told you that we would give someone else a chance to play Maria on two of the weekend performances?" Kirk asked.

Out in the audience, they were still applauding. "Yes," Taylor replied.

Kirk turned her around and pushed her back out on stage for a curtain call. "Forget it!" he shouted after her.

She looked back at him in the wings from center stage and smiled.

"There is no other Maria but you, Tay!" Kirk shouted to her from the wings.

Taylor was moved. She had never felt this happy before in her life.

But her happiness was short-lived.

On the last performance of the run, Kaylin missed her entrance and left Taylor alone on stage with no one to talk to. She had to improvise. She knew both parts and made it work and the audience never noticed, but after the show, she was terribly upset.

Kirk Cremer did not know what had happened and unfairly blamed it all on Taylor.

She could not believe he was blaming her. "Kaylin missed her entrance," Taylor explained to Kirk. "Didn't you notice?"

Kirk didn't move a muscle. Was she right? He hadn't noticed.

She stormed past him and left and he watched her go. "I-I guess not."

She found Kaylin backstage, standing dumbfounded near the table where she was playing cards. "I'm so sorry," she said. "I lost track of time."

Taylor glared at her. "He blamed me," she said, then turned and walked away.

Later that night, at the wrap party for *The Sound of Music,* Taylor did not hold back with the karaoke machine and sang a heart-wrenching version of

"Hopelessly Devoted" from the hit Broadway musical, *Grease,* originally sung by Olivia Newton-John. It was one of her favorite songs and after singing three weeks of "Do-Re-Mi" and "The Hills Are Alive with the Sound of Music," she wanted to show them she could do pop.

Kirk sat with his mother, Sandy, at a table and listened intently.

"Smart girl," Sandy said. "Singing a song from our next play. How did she know?"

"I told her," Kirk replied. "But like you said, she's a smart girl."

"What do you mean?" Sandy asked.

"She's a good listener and must have heard us talking because by the time I told her, she already knew," Kirk said and Sandy laughed.

Taylor was not done up on the stage and after the applause, Carly Simon's "You're So Vain" came up and Taylor belted it out, straight to Kirk.

Kirk squirmed. He knew she was still mad that he blamed her for Kaylin's missed entrance. She was right. He hadn't been paying attention. He should have been plugged in and he wasn't. It wasn't Taylor's fault *or* Kaylin's fault. It was his.

A few months later, *Grease* was BYTA's next play for the year and Kirk gave the lead role of Sandy to Taylor. Most say it is because she was light years ahead of the competition in the academy. Some say it was because Kirk's mom, also named Sandy, made him.

Some of the other kids in the company and their parents were not happy that, one more time, the tall blonde rich girl got the part. For Taylor, she was a natural, because her love of music was closer to pop and rock than to Broadway.

THIRTEEN

The weekend before *Grease* opened, Taylor spent the night at Kaylin's house. Taylor had all her things in an overnight bag. She grabbed her toothbrush and her high heels and headed for the bathroom. "Excuse me," she said and slipped on her high heels. "Practice makes perfect."

Kaylin giggled as Taylor sashayed into the bathroom and closed the door. "Always in character!" she shouted after her friend. Then she saw Taylor's diary resting on top of the stack of clothes in her overnight bag that was sitting on her bed. She scooted down to the end of the bed and picked up the diary.

When Taylor came out of the bathroom, Kaylin was lying in bed. "I didn't know you were jealous of me," she said.

Taylor stopped in her tracks. "How do you know that?" Then her eyes went to her overnight bag, where her diary was lying on top. "OMG! You read my diary!" She charged the bed and dove on it and wrestled Kaylin into a headlock. "Apologize! You traitor!"

Both girls started laughing uproariously. "I'm sorry! Ow! That hurts!" Kaylin shouted. "You deserve it! That was private!"

"Then why did you leave it on top of your stuff?"

Taylor grinned at her friend. "I don't have any secrets from you," she said and hugged her. "I wrote that because Kirk let you slide when you forgot your entrance and he blamed me. I thought he liked you better, that's all," she said.

Kaylin laughed. "You were right, though. I should've stood up for you. I'm so sorry I messed up. It was all my fault."

"No kidding! But I'm over it."

"Do you still think I'm better than you?" Kaylin asked.

Taylor thought about it, and laughed. "No way! I'm way better than you!"

The girls giggled.

Grease was another huge success, thanks to Taylor and Kaylin, and the Swift and Politzer families became fast friends. The wrap party was also a hit when Taylor got up on the stage. Everyone stopped what they were doing to listen. She belted out "Timber, I'm Falling in Love," made famous by country singer, Patty Loveless. The crowd went nuts and when she got off the stage, BYTA director, Kirk Cremer, and his mother, were waiting for her.

"Classic, Tay! Totally classic," Sandy gushed. "Thanks," Taylor said, fanning her face, drying it off. "I want to represent you," Kirk blurted out.

Taylor was surprised. "Represent me?" She wasn't sure what that meant.

Andrea Swift, who was nearby with her husband, overheard Kirk and came over.

"He wants to be your agent, honey," Andrea said. "Actually, I was thinking more like her manager,"

Kirk corrected.

"Really?!" she gushed. "That's so exciting!"

"Yeah and I have some great ideas! I'm gonna put you on the stage!" Kirk exclaimed.

Taylor's first gig as a singer was interesting and unexpected. The room was filled with Boy Scouts, surrounding the auditorium stage, all waiting for Taylor to sing "The Star-Spangled Banner." Taylor stood behind a microphone on the stage in the school auditorium and started singing. All the boys saluted at once.

In the back of the auditorium, Andrea and Scott Swift stood next to Sandy Wieder with their hands over their hearts. Scott and Andrea were amused that Taylor's big debut was a Boy Scout meeting. Sandy shifted awkwardly. "Well, it's a start," she whispered.

Andrea managed a polite smile in her direction and nodded, then gave her husband a wink. "I suppose you gotta start somewhere," she quipped.

The parents all shared a laugh.

When Taylor finished, the scouts, leaders, and parents all cheered wildly. She closed her eyes and smiled and took a bow.

FOURTEEN

Taylor held the last note of LeAnn Rimes' "One-Way Ticket" longer than she ever had before and all the wealthy teenage girls at The King of Prussia Mall went crazy. She took her bow and hopped off the stage and was immediately surrounded by them all. She happily greeted them and shook their hands and hugged them until Kirk rushed in, threw a coat over her shoulders, and whisked her away to the underground parking lot. "I just wanted to meet the kids!" Taylor shouted, looking back at the kids. "And they want to meet me!"

"No time," Kirk said. "We've got one more stop. I promised your mom I'd get you home early tonight. You're leaving for the Jersey shore."

"But I don't want to go!" Taylor pleaded. "I want to stay here. And sing! I'm on a roll! I don't want to go on hiatus!"

Kirk laughed. "Roll? Hiatus? Where are you getting this stuff?" he asked, opening the passenger's door.

She started to get in, then turned back to him. "From you," she said.

He laughed.

"This is going to be the worst summer of my life!" she said from the backseat.

"How could it be the worst summer?" Kirk said. "We're heading over to the Roadhouse. It's the last night of the contest. If you win, you get to open for Charlie Daniels at the county fair in September."

Taylor had been singing karaoke at the Roadhouse for a few months. It was the summer of 2001 and she was almost twelve years old.

Pat Garrett, the owner, was a country singer and she was a big fan of his music. "Plus, Kaylin and her family are going with you to Stone Harbor."

Taylor's eyes grew wide with excitement. "Kaylin's going?!" She liked the whole Politzer family.

"It's summer. After tonight at the Roadhouse, take a break. Have some fun," Kirk said. "But don't forget to wear sunblock."

Taylor thought about it for a moment. "Maybe I will," she said and tried to remain cool, but inside she was about to explode with excitement.

An hour later, Taylor bounced off the amphitheater stage of Pat Garrett's Roadhouse to thunderous applause. Kirk was waiting for her in the wings and hugged her. "Great job! You hear that?" he told her.

The applause continued even as he pulled her along toward the parking lot and his car.

"I think I nailed it," she said.

Kirk flashed her a grin. "I think you're right!" he said and opened the car door for her. "I'll call you in Stone Harbor and let you know if you won or not."

"Call me even if I don't," she said, getting into the car. "If it's bad news, I want to hear it from you."

"You got it," Kirk said and drove away.

A few hours later, the Politzers and the Swifts caravanned for two-and-a-half hours down to Stone Harbor on the Jersey shore. Kaylin and Taylor rode together and talked showbiz and acting the whole way.

The weather was perfect in Stone Harbor and the Swifts' new home on 112th Street across from the bird sanctuary was big, inviting, and roomy enough to accommodate two families. Cary, Kaylin's brother, hung with Austin and both boys planned on living on the beach. The grownups planned on spending their summer riding jet skis and soaking up rays.

The next morning, before any of the grownups or boys had awakened, Taylor was up looking at herself in her mirror. Her long blonde hair was all frizzedout and she was not happy. "Oh no!" she said.

Kaylin charged in, worried. "What's up?"

Taylor pulled at bundles of her hair. "Look! The ocean always ruins it."

"But we haven't even gone in the water yet," Kaylin replied.

"It's the sea air. It makes it all frizzy," she said, grimacing. Then she looked at her arm. "And look at my skin! It's all dry and crackly." She spun from the mirror and, as she passed a window, she caught a glimpse of something out the window and skidded to a stop. "Wait a sec," she said, suddenly deep in thought.

"What'd you see? A boy?" Kaylin kidded.

"The bird sanctuary?"

Taylor giggled. "No, look," she said and pointed at the empty lot a hundred yards up the street.

Kaylin looked. There was a large sandlot covered in blooming wildflowers. "Yeah? Flowers? So what? They're everywhere. They're beautiful."

"And they smell good. You know what our problem is? We need a special lotion for our skin. Happy skin, happy hair. It's gotta be designed for this environment down here."

"You mean the Jersey shore? Do you think our moms would let us walk into town and buy some?"

"No, that's not what I mean," Taylor said. "We should make our own. Out of the stuff that grows here, in Stone Harbor. It would be like part of the ecosystem or something, you know?"

"Not exactly," Kaylin said.

"Look. If it grows here and we do it right, it should fix the frizzes and dry skin problem. Because it's part of the environment down here."

Kaylin cocked her head. "I never thought of that before," she said. "But it makes sense."

Taylor turned from the window. "I think we should start a business."

"What are we gonna sell? De-frizzifier?" Kaylin asked.

"Yes! Shampoo. And lotion," she said and then looked out the window and nodded at the colorful sandlot down the road. "Out of those. All natural."

Fog obscured the water as Taylor and Kaylin walked along the boulevard running parallel to the shore. The large homes looked as if they were floating in the clouds. Taylor had a large net bag slung over her shoulder and they both carried pruning shears. "To capture the best scent, you gotta pick them early in the morning," Taylor said.

"Where did you hear that?" Kaylin asked. "HGTV," Taylor said.

They quickly reached the empty sandlot, blazing like a giant rectangular rainbow, blanketed in wildflowers. "Wow," Kaylin said. "Does it matter which color we choose?"

"I don't know," Taylor said. "My dad wanted to watch golf, so I had to turn it off." She shrugged. "Let's just take them all. If they smell good, grab 'em," she said and started snipping wildflowers with her pruning shears and shoving them into the net bag. "My mom has a mortar and pestle in the kitchen she uses to grind up spices." She started singing "Spice Up Your Life" by the Spice Girls and danced around the flowers. Kaylin took the bag from her and held it as her crazy best friend filled it with wildflowers, all the while singing and dancing to the beat in her head.

An hour later, Taylor dumped their net bag full of plucked wildflowers on the granite counter in her kitchen just as Andrea came down from upstairs, all sleepy-eyed and relaxed. "Good morn… ." She stopped herself when she saw the gigantic pile of wildflowers on the center island counter. She shot Taylor and Kaylin a look. She was determined not to suffer just because her daughter was constantly thinking and coming up with crazy schemes. So she just smiled.

"We're going into business," Taylor said and started chopping up the flowers and grinding them in the large stone mortar with the large stone pestle.

"Business. Well, that sounds like a good idea. Do you have a name for your company?"

"We were thinking of calling it 'Heaven Scent,'" Taylor said. "S-c-e-n-t, get it?"

Andrea nodded. "Good name," she said. She paused long enough to take in the scene—the flowers, the mortar and pestle, the bowl—then shook it all from her mind, poured a cup of coffee, and went past the girls and out the door to the porch. She plopped down on a lounge facing the ocean and the bird sanctuary. "Good luck!" she said.

Kaylin looked at Taylor and Taylor looked at Kaylin. "Your mom is cool," Kaylin said.

"Yeah," Taylor said and began grinding more flowers then dumping the ground-up pulp into a large bowl.

"I think I'll keep her." She poured mineral oil into the mixture of ground-up wildflowers. The mixture started changing. And bubbling. "Uh oh," Taylor said quietly.

"Heaven Scent is going to be the best perfumed body oil in America!" Kaylin said and took a deep whiff of the mixture and grimaced as if she had just smelled a dirty sock. "Well, maybe not the best yet, but it's getting there!"

"Heaven Scent," Taylor said dreamily, waved her hand over the mixture, and sniffed. "Ack!" she shouted and made a face. "More like garbage scent!"

Kaylin and Taylor shared a laugh, then both looked at each other and got worried. "This is not good," she said.

"I have an idea," Taylor said and raced out of the kitchen and up the stairs. She returned a minute later with a bottle of Bath and Body Works scented body oil. "This should help."

"But I thought we were marketing this as natural..." "I think we are going to go for semi-natural," Taylor replied.

"Good idea," Kaylin said and watched as Taylor poured Bath and Body Works oil into the mixture. It bubbled, burped, and turned the pulpy dead flowers into a dark, smelly, gooey mess.

They looked at each other. "I feel like crying," Kaylin said.

Taylor started laughing. "You know what this needs?" "What?" Kaylin asked.

"The Spice Girls!" Taylor said and dumped the whole thing down the kitchen drain. She turned and high-fived her friend and then both girls raced up the stairs, laughing. Moments later "Spice Up Your Life" by the Spice Girls, this time sung by the Spice Girls, blared from Taylor's stereo upstairs, loud enough that even Andrea, who was outside reading, could hear it. And of course, her daughter was singing along to it.

FIFTEEN

The boy next door was washing his parents' car when Taylor first noticed him. He had been over the previous night for a visit; his parents were friends with her parents and so she never paid any attention to him. But this was the first time she had *noticed* him. She watched him from the back veranda that faced the sea. Kaylin was watching the Stone Harbor Bird Sanctuary, which was visible from their vantage point. Taylor had binoculars and loved to come out on the veranda and look at the birds. In fact, minutes before, while watching a great egret, she heard someone humming and swung the binoculars around to find the sound. She found the boy next door soaping up his family's car. He had been in their house just hours earlier and she had not noticed him, but now she thought he was much more handsome than the egret or even the yellow-crowned night heron that populated the sanctuary. She thought he was dreamy. "I think to be entrusted with washing your daddy's expensive car, you gotta be pretty mature, don't you think?" she asked.

"I thought we were looking at birds," Kaylin said. "Gimme those," she said and snatched the binoculars away from her friend and trained them back on the bird sanctuary.

Taylor sighed and continued to watch the boy next door with her bare eyes.

It took Kaylin a minute or two to realize what was going on and she lowered the binoculars and watched her friend, then finally saw what, or rather who, she was looking at.

"Isn't that the boy who was over last night?" "Yep," Taylor said.

"We're too young," Kaylin said firmly and returned her attention to the birds.

"Too young for what? It's not like I was thinking o marrying him or anything, although I probably could." Kaylin lowered the binoculars slowly and glanced at Taylor. "Dude. Are you kidding me?"

Taylor glanced at Kaylin out of the corner of her eye and realized that what she had just said was *totally* ridiculous. She burst out laughing and Kaylin joined in.

Kaylin looked once more at the boy. "He *is* kind of cute, though."

That night the two families had dinner at Henny's, a local seafood restaurant on 3rd Avenue in downtown Stone Harbor. During the main course of fresh flounder, the bartender stepped out from behind the bar and sang "Yankee Doodle Dandy," accompanied by a karaoke machine. When he finished, there was a weak smattering of applause from the older patrons.

Taylor noticed there were quite a few teenagers in the restaurant, eating with their families, who did *not* applaud.

"Scott!" the restaurant manager shouted across the room and floated over to the Swift and Politzer table to speak to Taylor's dad. "How about that bartender?"

"Really good," Scott said.

"Thought we'd add a little patriotic flavor since the Fourth is coming." The manager was all captoothed smile and pinky-ring handshake. "Wow, have you grown!" he said to Taylor.

"Yes, sir, I have," she said. "Can I ask you a question?" Taylor asked him.

"Anything, honey," the manager said.

"Do you really think all these kids in here want to hear 'Yankee Doodle Dandy?'"

"Taylor!" Andrea said, mortified. "Let her speak," Scott said.

"Why do you say that, Taylor?" the manager asked, intrigued.

"Well, I notice you have a karaoke machine here and I thought maybe the kids would like to have a fresh face with their flounder," she said.

The manager burst out laughing. "Well, at least you know our menu."

"The flounder is my favorite! But what I'm trying to say is, how about you let me get up there and sing something on your karaoke machine. Got any country on it?"

The manager beamed at her. "Of course we do," he said. "Go for it."

Kaylin could not believe what Taylor was saying and when she got up, trotted up to the front of the room, and grabbed the mike, Kaylin almost died. Taylor did not waste any time and dialed in a song she knew on the karaoke machine.

The manager turned to Scott. "How *old* is she?" he asked.

"Eleven," Scott said and the manager said, "Sheesh," as he shook his head in amazement. Taylor started singing and the whole room grew quiet. It was a Faith Hill song. She rocked the house. When she finished, the whole restaurant burst into applause and cheers. Taylor flashed a bright smile and took a bow, then raced back to her seat, and let the manager push her chair in for her. She looked up at him. "How was that?"

"I got one question," he replied. "What?"

"When are you coming back?"

Everyone at the table laughed. Taylor laughed the loudest.

During dessert, the handsome boy who lived next door came over to their table to talk to Taylor. His family was at a booth across the room. They waved and Andrea and Scott waved back, then Scott turned to

Mr. Politzer. "Neighbors," he said by way of explanation.

Kaylin nudged Taylor who had not noticed the boy standing near her. When she looked up and saw him, she screamed.

Kaylin giggled.

"Hi, I didn't mean to scare you," the boy said. He seemed awkward and uncomfortable.

Taylor blushed. "You didn't scare me," she said, then didn't say anything for a long time.

"Well, I… I just wanted to tell you I think you are a good singer. A lot better than that old geezer behind the bar, singing 'Yankee Doodle Dandy.'"

Taylor nodded, unable to speak.

"Well," he said, and then shrugged. "See ya." He turned and started to walk away.

"When?" Taylor asked. She was a writer. If someone says they will 'see ya,' she wanted to know when that would be.

"T-Tomorrow?" he asked. He was suddenly nervous. "Sounds good," Taylor said and gave him a wink.

His eyes widened. He did not know what to do with that wink, so he spun on his heel, hightailed it out of there, and went back to his table.

Taylor turned to Kaylin. "Tomorrow, tomorrow, I love ya, tomorrow. You're always a day a-wayyyy!" She sang the song from their first play together, *Annie*. Then they both burst out laughing.

None of the grownups had a clue why their little girls were laughing.

After dinner at Henny's, they all stopped off at Springer's Ice Cream Parlor for cookies 'n cream ice cream. The girls took a separate table from the grownups and whispered to each other the whole time.

The next morning the boy next door came over as he promised, sat on the porch with Taylor and Kaylin, and talked about another girl he liked, who did not like him.

And asked for their advice.

Taylor could not believe it. She had almost thrown herself at him, as much as an eleven-year-old, turning twelve-year-old girl could, and all he wanted to talk about was the girl *he* liked.

Invisible, Taylor thought, after the boy had long gone. It's like I was *invisible.*

Taylor stayed inside the rest of the day. It was a perfect July day in 2001 and it was almost time to go back to Pennsylvania. Later that afternoon, bored out of her mind, after Kaylin came back from the beach, she turned on the big screen TV and they watched a repeat episode of *Behind The Music* starring the country-turned-pop star, Faith Hill.

"She's married to Tim McGraw," Taylor said, folding her legs under her on the chair. She always did this when she was excited about something. She knew all about her. "Look at her. She is so elegant!" she said.

When the show was over, Taylor could barely speak. "Did you hear what she said?"

"Not really," Kaylin said.

"She said the reason she got noticed was because she went to Nashville!"

"Yeah," Kaylin replied. "That makes sense." "Yeah," Taylor said, her mind wandering. "Why didn't I think of that before?"

Scott, Andrea, and Kaylin's parents came in from the beach, wrapped in towels and covered in sand. "You guys are still in here? We're going to have to start packing soon, so what do you want to do next?" Taylor turned to her mom with the biggest smile Andrea had ever seen. "Go to Nashville!"

Andrea looked at Scott and Scott looked at Andrea. "Oh God," Andrea said. "She's got that look in her eye, Scott." She knew whenever her daughter set her mind to something she would not let go until she accomplished it. That's just the way they taught her.

Taylor and her family returned home to Pennsylvania, full of energy and with high hopes for the remainder of the year. Every other word out of Taylor's mouth was Nashville. She could not stop talking about Faith Hill the whole way home. A lot was happening all at once.

She started middle school and turned twelve. The third BYTA play, *Bye-Bye Birdie,* began casting and she got the lead role of Kim MacAfee. Unlike the other leads she played, the part of Kim was nothing like her own personality. She thought it was a stretch and looked forward to it. When Kirk did not have a good part in the play for Kaylin, he made her his student director.

The songs were awesome and the play had been a huge hit on Broadway.

However, there was a problem at BYTA. It had been growing over the previous months, ever since Taylor arrived on the scene. The parents of the other children in the academy resented Taylor for always getting the lead. With *Bye-Bye Birdie,* they had had enough and stopped coming round. When they stopped coming, the money to fund the academy dried up. Kirk found himself forced to move the production to a smaller venue, but it was already too late.

After four performances, Kirk had to shut down

Bye-Bye Birdie; and not long after that, BYTA closed its doors for the last time.

A few weeks later, terrorists attacked New York on September 11 and changed the world.

SIXTEEN

Taylor watched her father stare at the news about the attacks on TV. She had never seen him look this scared. The world was changing so fast all around her and she dealt with it the only way she knew how: she wrote about it. No one noticed as she rushed upstairs, closed herself off in her bedroom, and dashed off a poem about 9/11. She felt better immediately.

After a while, her mom came in to say good night. "Mom?" Taylor said as her mom tucked her in. "Mmm?" Andrea said.

"Do you think I won the karaoke contest at the Roadhouse?" she asked.

"I hope so, sweetie," Andrea said, trying to put a good face on it.

"I think we need a vacation," Taylor said.

Andrea smiled down at her daughter. "And where would you like to go? As if I didn't already know."

"I hear Nashville is lovely this time of year," Taylor said.

Andrea knelt down and hugged her daughter. "We'll see," she said and kissed her good night.

"I could get a job at McDonald's," Taylor said. Andrea shook her head. "No way," she said. "Why not? Shania and Faith both worked at McDonald's when they went to Nashville." "I thought you wanted a job in music."

Taylor chuckled. "You said 'we'll see,'" she replied, drifting off. "That usually means yes."

Andrea backed out of the room. "You know me too well," she said. "Good night." She left the room and closed the door.

Taylor smiled at the doorway where her mom once stood. "That's true," she said softly and closed her eyes.

The next day, Andrea picked up Taylor from school as usual, and when they got home, Taylor saw that Kirk and his mother Sandy were waiting in their car out front. It was a chilly mid-September day and steam rose from the indoor pool and escaped through the sunroom vents.

Taylor hopped out of the car and ran to Kirk to hug him. "I didn't know if I was going to see you again!" she said. "You didn't call, so I guess I lost, huh?"

"I didn't want to spoil your fun at the beach," he said. "Yeah, I figured," Taylor said, trying to hide her disappointment as they all went into the house.

A few minutes later, they all sat down at the dining room table for coffee. Sandy looked at her son and nodded and Kirk got real serious. "Look, I am sorry I didn't call you. Mainly because I wanted to tell you in person. You won, Taylor. You won the contest!" Taylor screamed.

"Congratulations, Tay," Sandy said. "You open for Charlie Daniels at the Bloomsburg County Fair on the twenty-second!"

"Better get ready," Kirk said. "It's only a week away!"

Taylor turned to her mom. "And after the fair, we're driving to Nashville," she said. "Right?"

"We'll see," Andrea said.

"Yay!" Taylor said, then turned to Kirk. "'We'll see' means yes."

"Y-you're going to Nashville?" Kirk asked.

"She's never going to leave me alone unless we go," Andrea said.

"Well, I think that's a great idea!" Kirk said. "But you're going to need a demo. You're not going to Nashville empty-handed!"

"Right," Andrea said. "What's a demo?"

SEVENTEEN

Taylor sang "Big Deal" by LeAnn Rimes and the Bloomsburg County Fair crowd went crazy.

Who was this gorgeous white-blonde little girl belting out a LeAnn Rimes country classic? The song was about a girl who took a guy away from the singer and the singer is telling the gal she just got lucky. For Taylor it rang true. She followed the LeAnn Rimes song with a country favorite, "Timber, I Am Falling in Love" by Patty Loveless. The crowd loved her and she cemented herself in the psyche of the fairgoers.

Ronnie Cremer, Kirk's younger brother, was down front. He was a hard rock guitar player and a computer repairman. He owned a small repair shop on Lancaster Avenue in Kenhorst, Pennsylvania, about ten miles from where the Swifts lived. Behind his storefront, he had built a small recording studio where he produced artists' demos when asked. He had a serious interest in music, but it wasn't country.

Ronnie was hired by the Swifts to produce Taylor's first demo and he was ready for them when they arrived. He set up the karaoke machine and queued up the songs Taylor and Kirk had requested: "There's Your Trouble" by the Dixie Chicks, "One Way Ticket" by LeAnn Rimes, "Here You Come Again" by Dolly Parton, and as an afterthought, "Hopelessly Devoted" by Olivia Newton-John, because she sang it so well when she played Sandy in *Grease*.

Taylor picked the songs not just because she thought she sung them well, but because she felt them deep down inside her. They were all about the same thing— her hurt from that boy next door in Stone Harbor or her so-called friends at school who shunned her. More importantly, they were about her resolve to get over it. It took her hours to choose and it wasn't about the music first, it was about the words. And just like she put herself in the characters she portrayed in the plays she did at Berks County Youth Theater Academy, she put herself into the words of these songs. This was her demo and it had to be perfect.

When she stepped into the recording booth, she handed Ronnie a picture of her, taken by her neighbor at the farm, Andrew Orth. "Put this on the cover, please, along with a list of the songs," she said as she closed the door and checked the microphone. She looked through the glass and said something, but he didn't have the microphone on, so he potted it up.

"What'd you say, Taylor?" Ronnie asked. "Ready," she said.

Three hours later, when Taylor stepped out of the recording booth, Ronnie applauded. "That was totally awesome!" he said. "Do you play?"

"Play?" she asked.

"An instrument," he replied.

She thought about it. "No," she said. "Well, you should," he said.

"I was thinking of a 12-string. I've already got a 6-string," Taylor said.

Ronnie chuckled. He thought the girl had guts. "I don't know about a 12," he warned. "That might be too much for you right out of the gate."

"Ooo, never tell her she can't do something," Andrea said. "That's a surefire way that she's gonna do it."

Ronnie chuckled as he went back in the booth and played back the demo for them. They loved it. Ronnie laid the master digital files back to a CD master, made a stack of copies, and put them all in fancy jewel cases with a custom label with Taylor's picture on the cover. It looked very professional.

"You did a beautiful job, Taylor," Ronnie said.

They thanked him again and left, Taylor's first demo in hand.

The next day, Andrea packed their bags, piled her kids in the car, and aimed it toward Nashville, Tennessee. The plan was to hand out those CDs to record producers and get Taylor a big fat recording contract with a record label. But it didn't work out quite that way. This time.

EIGHTEEN

Taylor woke up. They were still driving home from Nashville. She rubbed the sleep from her eyes and stretched, leaning against the passenger door. She was still disappointed she did not get a record deal, but instead of it tearing her down, it gave her some ideas. "You awake?" she asked her mom.

"I hope so," Andrea said. "I'm driving."

They were almost home and they were looking forward to a nice hot bath and a home-cooked meal. They had driven all the way back from Nashville to Wyomissing Hills with nothing to show for it but a stronger resolve to succeed. At least that's how Taylor saw it. Nothing more than a bump in the road.

The whole family was back together for breakfast the next morning. "So what's next, Tay?" Scott asked.

"Two things, Daddy," Taylor said. "Learn the guitar, of course. And write my own songs."

"Atta girl, one foot in front of the other. Keep moving forward. I know how disappointed you must be," Scott said, finishing his coffee.

"Disappointed? I'm not disappointed. I got exactly what I needed in Nashville." She looked over at her mom and gave her a wink. "I want a new guitar. And make it a 12-string."

Andrea called Ronnie Cremer and asked him to come to the house. They needed help with a computer. It was running slow. Ronnie showed up within the hour and pulled into the driveway at the Swift mansion for the first time. His brother had told him it was nice, but he did not realize it was *this* nice. It was huge. He slung his computer bag over a shoulder and headed for the front door.

Andrea answered the door and flashed Ronnie a big smile. "Thanks for coming," she said, spotting his computer bag. "Oh, you won't need that, computer's all fast again. Must have fixed itself!" she said.

"All right," he said and started to leave.

"Wait," Andrea said. "Come in! While you're here, I want to see what kind of music teacher you are."

Ronnie finally put two-and-two together. "Oh! Great," he shrugged. "Okay."

They went upstairs to Taylor's floor.

A few minutes later, Ronnie sat on one chair and Taylor on the other. She had her six-string out and he was showing her the fingering for the G chord.

"Is a G chord a country chord?" Taylor asked.

"It's a chord-chord," Ronnie said. "I don't know too much about country."

"We'll make due," Andrea said from the doorway, then turned and left.

Taylor got her fingers into position. "They fit!" she said. "I got this guitar when I was eight, but my little fingers just wouldn't stretch. It is so cool! I thought I'd never be able to play!" She strummed the guitar. It was a kind of muted, off-key strum, but Ronnie helped her tune up the guitar and a couple of hours later, she strummed a perfect G chord. He taught her three chords that day and returned the next week and taught her three more. A few months later, Taylor was ready for the next step.

"Now let's put it together and make a song," Ronnie said. He had been coming twice a week for two months and Taylor was making good progress, he told Andrea.

"A country song?" Taylor asked.

"More like dance hall rock-and-roll," he said and started playing "I Want You to Want Me" by Cheap Trick and singing the lyrics.

When he was finished, Taylor clapped. "That is one of the most amazing songs I've ever heard! It's a classic, right?"

"Yes, it's one of my favorite songs," Ronnie replied.

Taylor grabbed the sheet music. "I can read this, you know," she said.

"You mean, I've been working with you all these months and you never told me you read music?"

Taylor shrugged. "I'm the student, you're the teacher. I learned it in music, at school," she said. She put the sheet music in front of her and played the chords and sang the lyrics. It was a bouncy rock tune. Earlier, Ronnie had explained about the structure of songs and pre-bridges and verses and bridges.

About halfway through playing the song she stopped. "That's the way they did it right?"

"Yeah," Ronnie said. "That's the way it's played." He wasn't sure what she meant.

"Mind if I make a few changes?" "Changes?" What was she getting at? "I have an idea," she said.

Ronnie shrugged. "Go for it."

Taylor started playing the song from the beginning again, except this time, in a much slower, country tempo. She sang, *I want you to want me, I need you to need me, I'd love you to love me, I'm begging you to beg me.* She sang the song all the way through with the new country phrasing and tempo. It had a completely different feeling and meaning the way she sang it, Ronnie thought, and when she finished, he applauded. "Wow!"

"I want to be a country singer, Ronnie," she said. "Not a dance hall rock star." She flashed him one of her bright smiles. "At least not yet. I'm only twelve."

Ronnie laughed. "See ya next week," he said and left.

That night, Taylor wrote her first song. It was called "Lucky You." She used some of the chords Ronnie taught her, except she mixed them around. First a C, then a D, then a G. She heard the melody in her head. She was afraid she was going to forget it so she hummed it over and over until it was stuck in her head. Then she wrote the words for the first stanza and hummed along. It was late. The door creaked open and Andrea came in. "What's that, Tay-tay?" she asked.

"Writing a song," she said. She was on her bed in her pajamas with her guitar and a notebook open in front of her. She wrote some more down, then smiled at her mom.

"What's it about?" Andrea asked.

"Grandma Margie," Taylor answered, writing something else down. "Mom?"

"Yes, sweetie?"

"Do you think Grandma's friends thought she was different because she was a singer?"

"You mean like your friends at school?"

"Yeah," Taylor said and blushed. "I guess that's true." "Sing it for me," Andrea said and sat on the side of the bed.

"It's called 'Lucky You,'" Taylor said and sang the song for her mom. When she was done, Andrea hugged her.

"Do you think there's a place where the kids aren't mean to me?" Taylor asked.

"There's gotta be, honey," Andrea soothed. "God didn't put you here to suffer."

"I guess not," Taylor replied. "He wants you to be happy."

"I am, Mama," she said and hugged her mother again. "The guy in Nashville was right. No one's interested in demos of karaoke songs. They want originals."

"You're probably right," Andrea replied. "You know what else?"

"What's that?"

"How much money do you spend on my music?"

"A LOT!" Andrea shot back.

"In Nashville, all the record companies said I had to be eighteen. But that's because they don't know there are girls out there just like me who want their own music. And their mamas buy it for them."

"Yeah? Where did you get all this information?"

"From the kids. I hear them talking." She picked up her guitar again and strummed a chord. "The fact that she's different and yet she's the same..." She sang the line from her song. "I know I'm different because you and Daddy are rich and me and Austin get everything we want."

"Oh come on, honey, that's not true," Andrea said. "Yes, it is," she said. "The kids know we are wealthy and some of them hate me because of it. But I love country music and lots of them do too and that means I'm the same as them. And they're gonna beg their mamas to buy them records just like I begged mine."

"I think you got something there," Andrea said. "What are you gonna do? Write songs and go back to Nashville? You better start begging me now, because it's gonna take a lot more this time than the last time.

"I'm not thinking about that," Taylor replied. "I'm thinking about giving the kids the music they want."

Andrea smiled at her daughter. "Grandma isn't the only one that should be nicknamed Lucky."

Taylor shook her head. "Maybe Grandma was nicknamed Lucky, but I don't need luck," she said and strummed the first chord. "Want to hear it again?"

"Please," Andrea said.

NINETEEN

When Taylor finished writing "Lucky You," her mom and dad finally broke down and bought her a 12-string guitar.

"Ronnie's going to say something," Andrea kidded. "Until he hears me play it," Taylor retorted. "Twice the strings, twice the fun!"

A few weeks later, Andrea heard the sounds of guitars coming down from upstairs. It was still early in the morning and the music had been constant for hours. The music was so full, it almost sounded like two guitars. She hurried up the stairs and went into the room. "Tay, who is up here with you?" she asked.

Taylor laughed. "It's just me and my 12-string, Mom!" she grinned broadly.

A little while later, Andrea found her in the bathroom, taping up the fingers on her left hand. "What are you doing?!" she asked.

"Taping up my fingers," Taylor said, wiggling her fingers. "They got all bloody. From the strings."

The next day at school, Kaylin and Taylor walked into the gym together. "Listen, just follow my lead," Kaylin said as they stepped out onto the basketball court.

The women's basketball coach was already there with her assistant, holding a ball. "Let's see the tall one," she whispered. "Hey blondie! Think fast!" the coach said and bounced the ball to Taylor.

Taylor tried to catch it, but it flew right past her.

The coaches looked at each other. "Oh boy," the assistant said.

"Sorry!" Taylor said. "I wasn't ready." "No problem, Swift," the coach said.

One of the other kids had gone and retrieved the ball and threw it to her and she caught it expertly. She gently handed the ball to Taylor. "Let's see you rush down court and sink one."

Taylor looked over at Kaylin and pleaded with her eyes: get me out of here. But she gave it a shot. She ran down the court holding the ball and when she got within striking distance of the basket she threw the ball and it sailed at a 90-degree angle to the net and got stuck in the third row of the bleachers. "Oops!" she cried.

Later, outside the gym, as Taylor and Kaylin walked to class, they had a heart-to-heart. "I can't do it, Kay. I'm a total spaz," Taylor said.

Kaylin giggled. "Well, I can't disagree with you there. You've got the height so I thought basketball would be the perfect sport for you."

"It's not just that," Taylor countered. "I'm just not into it. All I ever think about is music. To me, going out for a sport just feels like it is taking time away from what I really want to do. You know, the stage, music. All that stuff we went through together at BYTA?"

Kaylin nodded and Taylor saw the sadness in it. They were best friends suddenly at cross purposes. "I know you want to go out for sports. I know you're sick of acting and the whole thing."

Kaylin hugged her friend. "To me it just got ugly at BYTA. I'd rather do something else."

They came to a place in the path where one sidewalk led to Kaylin's class and the other led to Taylor's and they stopped there. "What are you going to do?" Taylor asked.

"Track and field," Kaylin replied without hesitation. They looked at each other for a moment. "All right,"

Taylor finally said. "So, I'll see you later then?"

Kaylin thought about it for a moment, then nodded. "Sure," she said, then started trotting toward the sports field.

Taylor watched her go and knew in her heart that when the Berks Youth Theatre Academy went under, their constant companionship went with it. She headed for homeroom and when she walked into class and down the row of desks to her own, a couple of the girls snickered when they saw her fingers all taped up. She already missed Kaylin, but she knew she had to follow her dreams. Although they saw each other every day in school, from that day on, Kaylin was always busy with sports, and Taylor drove herself to succeed in the music business.

At lunch, Taylor went to a table she had sat at for the first month since starting middle school. Kaylin wasn't there. She was out on the field, running track. There were some girls she knew from her classes, so she sat down with her cafeteria tray, loaded with the best the school had to offer. One girl sized her up and said, "Hey, beanpole," as she got a look at her expensive hot lunch. "Why are you here? You sure you're in the right school? This ain't a private academy, you know." You could tell who was rich and who was poor by what car they were dropped off in and what they had for lunch.

Most kids were either eating out of sack lunches or did not have any lunch at all. The school provided free lunches, but there were a number of girls who would have none of the charity. They were too proud.

"What do you mean, why am I here?" Taylor asked. "I... I'm here because I *want* to be here."

"Sorry, beanpole, no one *wants* to go to Wyomissing" another girl said. That's what the students called Wyomissing Area Junior Senior High School because the real name was a mouthful. "*Especially* someone from the Hill!" That's what they called Wyomissing Hills— the Hill. Taylor knew what they were getting at. There was always a wide gap at the school between the rich and the poor and she never played that game. People were people to her. But not everyone at school thought the way she did.

"But it's a public school. *Any*one can go."

All the girls laughed. "Jeez, can you get any dumber?

Oh, by the way—nice fingers," one of them said and they all laughed again.

Taylor tried to join in the laughter and wiggled her fingers. "Guitar lessons. I guess I overdid it," she said. "They got bloody because I practice too much. Hey, I'm being rude. Do you guys want any of this?" she asked, pointing to her tray packed with lots of food. "I have plenty."

One short girl gave her a derisive look. "We don't need your charity, rich girl," she said, got up, and looked around the table. "Coming?"

All the girls got up at once and went to another table, leaving Taylor alone. She watched them for a moment, then tried to eat. She bit her lower lip to keep from crying, then took a deep breath and stood and walked over to them. "You know, I can't help it if my mom and dad are rich. But still, they always taught me to share." Then she turned her back on them and walked away.

"Don't let the door hit you in the butt on the way out, country girl," one of the girls shouted after her and the girls all laughed again.

Taylor stopped and turned back and glared at them. "Thanks. When I have my first concert, I'll make sure you get front row seats," she said and went back to her lunch.

A few months later, in April of 2002, Taylor walked out onto another basketball court. The Philadelphia 76ers' home court. She took center stage and sang "The Star-Spangled Banner." She had tears in her eyes. This was a championship game. The NBA finals.

With a sellout crowd of more than 20,000. When she finished, she waited for the applause and closed her eyes and knew one more time it was worth it. She nodded her head and turned to leave and there was the famous rapper, Jay-Z, sitting courtside. He stuck his hand out and high-fived her as she walked by. "Beautiful," he said. Taylor realized who he was as she was walking away and her eyes grew as wide as saucers.

She floated off the court and did not remember to breathe again until she was well past the snack bar and into the arms of her proud mother, who was waiting for her. "Beautiful!" Andrea gushed. "Just beautiful!" "That's exactly what Jay-Z said to me!" Taylor gushed right back and giggled and showed her mom her hand. "LeAnn touched this one," she said, holding out one hand. "And this one got touched by Jay-Z!" she said and held out the other. "That's gotta mean something."

"It means you're on your way," her mom replied.

TWENTY

The year Taylor became a teenager, she had already written over 50 songs, most of them about relationships and experiences. She begged her mother for another road trip to Nashville. Andrea agreed. Eventually, the trips became a regular, monthly ritual. Then on one trip, they visited the Nashville Music Hall of Fame and Taylor heard the words she had been waiting to hear her whole life.

At one exhibit, she pushed the button and the late country folksinger, Gordon Lightfoot, spoke to her from a small speaker behind his gigantic picture. "You don't have to be the best, you just have to do the most."

Taylor realized what she had to do. She had to do more.

A few weeks later, around the supper table, her father had something to say about that. "I don't get it. Quantity not quality? That just doesn't seem like a good lesson to me," he said.

Taylor stopped eating for a moment, then looked her dad in the eye. "It can be both, but it doesn't have to be. You can also get great by getting out there," she said and went back to her supper. "For me, if I don't get out there, it's *not* gonna happen."

"Makes sense to me," Andrea said. "Marketing.

Guess I know a little bit about that."

"I should get out there and do more shows," Taylor said.

Scott thought about it and smiled at his daughter. "All right. Let me see what I can do."

That night, Taylor sat on the front porch and waited.

When her father's car pulled into the driveway, she hurried over, opened the door for him, and took his briefcase to carry it in the house for him. "Wow!" he said. "I don't even get this kind of great service from the valet parkers in the building!"

"What do you have for me, Daddy?" she asked as they walked toward the house.

Scott grinned and shook his head in wonderment. "How do you always know when I have something for you?"

Taylor shrugged. "I don't have to know, Daddy. You just always do."

"Yeah, okay, you got me," he said. "It's a gig."

Taylor sucked in a breath.

"They want you to sing the anthem at the U.S. Open."

"The U.S. Open!" Taylor bounced around then stopped. "What's the U. S. Open?"

Scott chuckled. "It's a golf tournament."

Taylor's enthusiasm slowed to a crawl. "Oh, okay, golf," she said.

"Not just golf. The biggest golf tournament in the world," he added. "Millions of people will be watching."

Taylor thought about it for a moment. "Oh my God, that's *huge!*" she squealed and hugged him tight, dropping his briefcase.

Scott chuckled some more, picked up his briefcase, and dusted it off.

"I think it should be 'America the Beautiful,'" she said straight-faced.

Scott gave her a look. "Why?"

"Because I have a feeling that's what everyone wants to hear," Taylor replied.

"I'll see what I can do," Scott said. No sense arguing with her. She had always known what she wanted and what the audience wanted too.

A month later, Taylor finished singing "America the Beautiful" to rousing cheers from the huge audience

of spectators at the U.S. Open Golf Tournament in Atlanta. She ran offstage and right into the arms of her father. "That was absolutely beautiful," he said. "Listen to that." The crowd was on their feet cheering and Taylor smiled.

"I want you to meet someone," Scott said and stepped aside, revealing a man standing behind him, smiling broadly at Taylor. "Beautiful singing, Taylor.

I loved it! I think you have a lot of talent," he said and offered his hand and she shook it. "I'm Dan Dymtrow," he said. "I represent Britney Spears."

"Oh my God," Taylor whispered.

"And I want to represent you," he said. "Here's what we do. I know Steve Migliore. Ever heard of him?"

Taylor nodded quickly, trying not to show how excited she was.

"We get Mr. Mig over at Sigma Studios in Philly to produce a professional demo and then we get you to Nashville permanently once I land you a job there. Might take a year. How does that sound?"

"It sounds like you've been reading my mind," Taylor retorted and everyone laughed. She knew all about Steve Migliore. He was a legend, known as the behind the-scenes genius for a lot of multi-platinum hit pop singles.

A month later, when Taylor played "Smokey Black Nights" for the first time for Steve at Sigma Studios in Philadelphia, her father was shocked because he could not remember ever hearing it before. "When did you write *that?!*" he asked.

"At the shore," Taylor said. "I was 11."

The lyrics were about walking through smoky black nights with a broken heart. "When did she have a boyfriend?" Scott whispered, taking Andrea aside.

"Never, silly," Andrea whispered back.

"Then what's with those lyrics?" he asked a little too loud and Taylor heard him.

"Dad, what do you think? I haven't even kissed a boy yet!" Taylor said.

Scott blanched.

Steve chuckled. "So what *are* the things you write about, Tay?" Steve asked. "All your songs are about relationships and experiences about love."

Taylor shrugged. "They're about what I'm feeling. Also, I write about what I *want* to happen. Sometimes, what I *hope* will happen."

Taylor's new demo took a week to produce and included polished versions of two of her favorite songs that she had written: "Lucky You" and "Smokey Black Nights." Dan Dymtrow's Madd Talent Agency out of New York City was the rep. Steve was a pop producer, not a country producer, so although he managed to capture the country, he also added his own pop style and the result was unique to Taylor. When she finished the vocals for "Smokey Black Nights," Steve came into the booth to adjust things for one more take.

"Steve?" Taylor asked.

Steve tightened down a mike stand and moved it closer to her. "Yeah?"

"You recorded LeAnn, didn't you?"

"I sure did, and Madonna and Bowie and even Whitney Houston."

Taylor's eyes grew wide. "Can they hear us out there?" she asked, referring to her family and the other engineers in the studio.

Steve flicked a switch. "Now they can't."

"How was I? I know my daddy paid for this, but, really, how was I?"

"Tay, you are the best of the best, no kidding. I don't need the money. Just like you want to create something good, so do I. And I think we just did."

Taylor hugged him tight. "Thank you," she whispered.

Dan Dymtrow booked Taylor for a lot of singing gigs and invited her to Britney Spears' camp for performers, where Britney helped underprivileged kids get closer to their dreams. Steve Migliore praised Taylor to whomever would listen during the intervening months and Taylor's trips to Nashville finally paid off. In September of 2003, RCA, the label that signed Elvis Presley in the 1950s, heard her demo and offered her a development deal. She was in the eighth grade and the bullies at Wyomissing Area Junior Senior High were left in the dust as she ignored them and concentrated on her writing. In honor of them making her life a living hell, she gave them a gift: a song she wrote about them when she was twelve entitled "The Outside."

TWENTY ONE

The monthly trips to Nashville were over. In April of 2004, Sony/ATV, the music and publishing parent company of the RCA Records label, had gotten wind of Taylor's development deal with one of their labels and offered Taylor a paid job writing songs and working with their staff songwriters. She had just turned 15. It impressed everyone around her.

For Taylor it was great to have two jobs—at RCA and Sony. But where was the album? She was already 15. LeAnn had recorded a record at 13. And that's what Taylor wanted: to make an album. The Swifts moved to Hendersonville, Tennessee, a suburb of Nashville, to help Taylor fulfill her dream.

A couple of weeks before they left for Nashville, the Swifts paid a final visit to the man who first gave Taylor a shot: country music legend Pat Garrett. He was in his office signing checks when all four Swifts drifted into the room. "Oh my God, I got everyone here," Pat said, smiling. "To what do I owe this very pleasant surprise?"

"Well," Scott said. "We just wanted to let you know that we're going."

"Well, that's nice," Pat said. "Where you heading?" "Nashville," Scott replied.

"Oh, great place for a vacation!" Pat said. "How long for?"

"For the rest of our lives," Scott replied. "What?!" Pat said.

"That's what you told me to do!" Scott said.

Pat scratched his head. "Well, yeah, I did tell you that, but I never expected you to listen! No one ever does!"

They all laughed.

Prior to leaving, Dan Dymtrow had hustled some work in Nashville for Taylor and got her an offer from Abercrombie & Fitch to be the face of an upscale casual line of clothing known as *Rising Stars*. Taylor was a rising star in Nashville and they wanted to plug her into their line. She would be plastered all over a 19-page spread in *Vanity Fair*.

"What do you think?" Dan asked. "Will you do it?"

"I'm not cool enough for this," Taylor said. "I mean, this is Abercrombie & Fitch!"

"I thought you wanted to get out there," Andrea said. Taylor thought about it, then smiled. "I'll do it."

Taylor registered at Hendersonville High School and started the ninth grade. It was a completely different experience for Taylor than junior high in Wyomissing.

The city of Nashville was the music capital of the world and the schools there were all about the music biz. For Taylor, it was the first time her school experience was a happy one. She was going to high school and had a job with Sony Records.

On her first day of school, she met a girl in English class. "Hi," Taylor said to her as she sat down at the desk behind her.

"Hi, good ta see ya, eh?" Abigail answered in a perfect Minnesota accent.

Taylor did a double-take. "Are you from Minnesota?"

"Napoleon Dynamite," Abigail replied, shaking her head.

Taylor squealed with delight and the entire class stopped for a beat to look, then went back to their business.

"I *love Napoleon Dynamite,*" Taylor whispered, also in a perfect Minnesota accent.

"It touches my heart," Abigail whispered with a wink.

"Mine too!" Taylor said. "You an outsider too?" "Of course! Hey, speaking of hearts, how's your love life?"

Taylor giggled. "*What* love life?" she replied. "I hear ya," Abigail said. "Mine sucks too."

That's when Taylor saw the boy in the next row. "Then again..." she let it trail off.

"Brandon Borello," Abigail explained. "Player."

Both girls shared a laugh. Abigail turned around and stuck out her hand. "Abigail Anderson," she said.

Taylor took her hand. "Taylor Swift."

"Great name," Abigail replied. "Ladies and gentlemen, Taylor Swift!" she said a little too loudly and received a few chuckles from the class.

"That's how it's gonna be done, dude!" Taylor said in her normal voice.

"Okay, but in a Minnesota accent, please," Abigail scolded.

"Ohhh, sorryyy," Taylor said, back to her Minnesota accent.

Taylor took out her phone and sang a short melody into it then clicked it off, just as the teacher stepped into the room.

"Jeez, you're a singer, aren't you? I thought you were a model," Abigail said.

"Writer," Taylor said. "I write stories. And I sing them. How about you?"

"Champion swimmer," Abigail said. "Oh, that's great!" Taylor said. "Someday," Abigail finished.

Taylor laughed. It was the first time she had laughed in a school. She liked this girl.

TWENTY TWO

Taylor and Abigail talked like that for a year and were inseparable. Taylor finally met Brandon and discovered they had one thing in common—they both liked Tim McGraw. That was the start of a beautiful relationship. But Brandon wound up cheating on her during that year and they eventually broke up.

Taylor managed the pain of the breakup through her job at Sony. Every day after school, Andrea waited for her outside and drove her to her songwriting job at Sony. Taylor had her own room and worked with other songwriters and sometimes even blended in their lyrics and melodies with her own. But not often. The older and more established songwriters were polite, but thought of Taylor as a kid.

One day, Andrea dropped Taylor off at her office after school and Taylor took the stairs up to the second floor, two at a time. She passed Troy Verges' office and Brett Beavers' office, passed the Warren Brothers, and Liz Rose and went into her own room. It was tiny and had a guitar and a piano and a small window overlooking the back of the building. She sat down in a chair and puffed out a breath. "This is where I'm supposed to be inspired?" she thought.

Liz Rose peeked her head in. "Heard you singing yesterday. It was nice," she said.

"Thanks," Taylor said.

"Maybe we'll work together some time," Liz said. "You'd be the only one who would," Taylor said.

"No one here wants to. Doesn't matter about my songs or my music. They only care about my age. It isn't fair."

"I know, sweetie," Liz said in her distinctive Texas drawl. "Life *ain't* fair. Tell you what, though. Here's how I handle it with other writers when I help them: I pick your brain then I make you spill your guts," she said and winked. Liz liked her. This girl wrote with sincere vulnerability, but she was also tough. Plus she had the voice of youth, something Liz wanted now that she was over 30.

"Let's try some stuff together," Taylor said. Liz was honest and not full of bull like the others.

"Your first good decision since you got here," Liz chided and both of them laughed.

"Okay, let's say we do something good. How do we get it down?"

Liz grinned and pulled up the blinds on the window.

Out in back of the building was a small shed. "Out there. Best country producer in town. They call it the Pain in the Art Studio."

Taylor giggled and looked. It was a shed. But it had phone wires and electrical wires going to it. "Really?"

"Nathan Chapman. He's got everything we need in there. He'll be cutting the tunes, don't you worry."

At that moment, Nathan Chapman stepped out of the shed and stretched. He was tall with red thinning hair and a winning smile. He looked up and saw Taylor staring down at him and waved. Embarrassed, she let the blinds drop. "Oh my lord, I think he saw me staring down at him."

"He already knows who you are, honey. He's just waiting for us to give him something to do," Liz said, then remembered something. "Oh! I almost forgot! Come to the Bluebird Café," she said. "Tuesdays are open mike night. They'll give you a slot. You sing a few songs. You're pretty enough and tall enough to pass. I'll try to get some mucky-mucks to show up and hear ya. You never know."

"The Bluebird," Taylor said and remembered the day she saw it for the first time. It seemed like an eternity ago. She had promised herself that she would play there one day. "Are you saying I can play there?"

"Of course you can," Liz said.

Taylor was floating in the clouds when she got home that night. But there was a phone call waiting for her. From RCA. Andrea handed her the receiver.

Taylor listened for a minute. "But what about my record deal?" she asked.

Andrea heard the disappointment in her tone. "Okay, thank you," Taylor finally said politely and hung up. She turned around and faced her mother, brushing away her tears.

"What did they say?" Andrea asked and came over to her daughter, comforting her.

"They want to put me on the shelf for another year instead of letting me record," Taylor sighed. "Then they'll see what develops after that. They think I'm too young to make a record."

"What?!" Andrea was angry, seeing her daughter was crestfallen.

"Go away and come back when you're 18," Taylor continued. "That's what they *said*." She felt bitter; she had sent them scores of songs and had not received one bite.

"Oh honey, I'm so sorry," Andrea said. "What do you want to do?"

"Call Dan and tell him I quit," Taylor said. "Whoa, wait a minute, honey. RCA is a big record label," Andrea replied.

"They don't know how good I am," she replied. "I'll stay with Sony publishing and keep working on writing songs because it's fun. But RCA is not going to produce my album. They just want to put me on the shelf and keep me from making one with somebody else. That's not fair. I want to find someone else. Someone who believes in me as much as I believe in me," she said, then turned on her heel, stormed out, and ran up the stairs to her room.

TWENTY THREE

T aylor stared at the blue awning for an eternity before her mother said a word. "Well, I gotta admit," Andrea said, finally breaking the silence. "You sure called it." They were looking at the front of the Bluebird Café, just across the strip mall parking lot on Hillsboro Pike in Nashville. There was a short ramp leading up to the front door and Taylor thought it looked like the red carpet at the Grammys, even though it was not red.

Taylor looked at her mom and dad and smiled. "Pat was right. There're only two reasons why I'm here. Me and you." She hugged her, then opened the car door, grabbed her guitar case from the backseat, and got out. Andrea and Scott got out the other side and they crossed the road and entered the Bluebird Café.

There was a long line of people waiting to get in, but Liz Rose was waiting for them at the door and let them in immediately. The place was filled with lights and ceiling fans and tables and a bar along the back. The walls were filled with photographs of Nashville's greats. On the right side when you walked in was a small band riser with a set of drums and a bunch of mics.

The place filled up quickly and Taylor got called up for her set just as fast. "Ladies and gentlemen, put your hands together for a new gal in town, who has been writing songs with those geezers over at Sony— Taylor Swift!"

Taylor did a quick check of the tune on her guitar, then while the capacity crowd applauded, she crossed the room and hopped up on the riser and got behind the mic. Dan had told her the place was packed with record label luminaries and it gave her the jitters. But she knew the best way to calm down was to start playing. "This is my first time playing at the Bluebird," she said, cool as ice. She opened with her own song, "Writing Songs About You," and had them from the first downbeat.

She did a short acoustic set of her own songs and while she played, there was one guy with long hair in the audience who couldn't take his eyes off her, as he sat and scribbled into a notebook.

When she finished and stepped off the stage, the man with the long hair stood up, hurried over to her, and blocked her path. He knew he only had a few seconds to make his pitch and so he spoke fast. "Taylor, there are a lot of important people here tonight, myself included, but I just wanted to tell you that I think I see what you are going for and I can make that dream come true." He handed her his business card. She read it while he introduced himself. "My name is Scott Borchetta. I was with UMG and I'm starting up a new record label and I want to sign you. I know all about you and RCA; I did my homework. I know you were unhappy and I know I can change that. I will make your first album. Can we talk?"

Taylor didn't even have time to put her pick between the strings of her guitar. She craned around and found her mom and dad at a table near the back. "Sure," she said, trying to remain calm. She liked his honesty.

"Follow me." She weaved through the tables to find her parents and Andrea and Scott stood up and each gave her a hug. "This is Scott Borchetta," Taylor said, reading off the business card he gave her as she sat down between her mom and dad. "He was with UMG and now he's starting up a new label."

"Have a seat, Scott," Andrea said and waved him to a chair and Borchetta sat down. "What's on your mind?"

"Well, I have good news and bad news," Borchetta said calmly and turned his attention to Taylor. "The good news is I want to sign you to a record deal."

"And the bad news?" Andrea asked.

"The bad news is I'm no longer with Universal Music Group Records," he replied.

"Then why are we talking?" Andrea asked. "You want to make a record deal with my daughter without a record label?"

"Look, I've been around the block a few times. I grew up in the business, my father was a big record promoter on the West Coast, and I've worked for a few labels including MTM Records and MCA Records and helped launch DreamWorks Nashville. I know how to do this."

"All right," Taylor said. "What's your plan?"

"I know this sounds unfair because you don't know me from Adam, but I want you to wait for me. I'm working on something big. I've done a lot of research on you, Taylor, and I think you are going to want to be a part of it."

He shifted his gaze to everyone and continued. "I have a business plan and tons of interest from the industry. Taylor's material taps into an audience the country and pop world has been ignoring: teenage girls. And their moms."

Taylor lit up.

Borchetta smiled. "First off, complete creative control. If you want your first album to be all your own songs, you got it," he said.

Behind them, Liz Rose took the stage and began her set, singing and playing her own songs.

"You see that woman up there?"

"Sure," Borchetta said. "That's Liz Rose, the songwriter. Works for Sony. Do you know her?"

"She's the reason I'm here. We've been working together. She's been teaching me how to make my songs better—and I think they are. I want to be able to use our songs."

Borchetta flashed a grin. "You got it."

Taylor studied her mom's and dad's eyes and saw they were waiting for her. It was exactly what she wanted. Independence. And Scott Borchetta was promising it. She smiled at Scott and stuck out her hand. "Okay, Scott Borchetta. I'll wait for you."

"Thank you!" Borchetta said taking her hand, then looking at Andrea and Scott Swift. "It's gotta be okay for you too."

Scott Swift smiled. "My daughter has excellent instincts and she is also an excellent judge of character. Get your label going. But don't take too long or we won't be there when you come calling."

"Thank you!" Borchetta gushed.

"What are you gonna call it? Scott Swift asked. "Your new label? I want to see your business plan. I may want to buy a stake in it."

"Big Machine Records," Borchetta replied.

TWENTY FOUR

On September 1, 2005, Labor Day, Scott Borchetta kept his word and launched Big Machine Records. He set up shop on Music Row in downtown Nashville, Tennessee. Because of his close ties with Universal Music Group, UMG signed on to distribute all of Big Machine's content, with the publishing rights going to Sony/ATV. Taylor would be one of the label's first artists and they would produce her first album.

She was 15 years old.

Borchetta looked up from his desk when Taylor walked into the room with her guitar under her arm. "I want to play you something," she said. "Liz helped me with it."

"Let's hear it," Borchetta said and offered her the usual chair opposite his desk.

She sat down and played "Tim McGraw." When she finished, Scott had tears in his eyes.

"Tay, you never cease to amaze me. Where on earth did that song come from?"

Taylor shrugged. "From inside me. I thought of it in math class," she said and Borchetta laughed. "It's about me and Brandon. That's the guy I liked when I was a freshman. We didn't have a song, so this is a song about us having one."

Borchetta laughed again. "Not life as it is, but life as it should be," Borchetta said.

Taylor laughed. "I sang it at the talent show last year at school and the kids loved it. Liz helped me make it better," she said.

"Sounds like a single to me. I'm glad you're here. There are some people coming over for a meeting."

There was a knock on the door. "Come!" Borchetta shouted and the door opened and two men came in. Nathan Chapman sported a red beard, a New York Yankees cap, and aviator sunglasses. "Tay, you already know Nathan Chapman. You asked, he came. He has agreed to help you produce your album. Best producer country music has to offer, but I'm guessing you already know that since it was your idea to bring him in."

"I'm so happy you're coming aboard!" Taylor said and hugged Nathan.

"And this is your new manager," Borchetta said and the other man went over to Taylor and shook her hand.

"Rick Barker," he said, introducing himself.

"Dan's okay with me getting a new manager?" Taylor whispered to Scott.

"He's cool. He knows the deal. We keep the management in house."

"Okay," Taylor said, but Barker heard the uncertainty in her tone.

"Look, I get that you just met me and don't know anything about me, but I have a question for you. Do you want to sell 500,000 albums?" Barker asked her.

"Heck, yeah!"

"Then you have to meet 500,000 people," Barker replied.

Taylor thought about it for a long moment. "I never thought about it that way," Taylor said. "But it makes sense. Most artists sell records and get their fans. You're saying, let's get some fans, and they'll buy my records." "That's exactly what I'm saying," Barker said. "Okay, Rick. But where are you gonna find me 500,000 fans?" Taylor asked.

"We have big plans. First, we'll find those fans by putting you on the radio. We'll start in California. We're going to San Diego and we'll work our way up north. I'm going to introduce you to every country station manager and personality from San Diego to Eureka and we're going to give them your new demo and they're going to see your pretty smiling face and your creative brilliance and they're going to go nuts for your music and for you. And when we leave, they are gonna start talking about you." Barker said. "And once everybody is talking about you and the public hears some new original songs, they're going to start asking for more. Then we give them a gift—your first album."

Taylor flashed a smile. "Let's do it!"

When summer break came around, Rick Barker drove and Taylor rode shotgun in his red Suburban SUV. Andrea was in the backseat navigating. They drove to San Diego and almost lived out of that car for weeks, hitting the radio stations and handing out hundreds of demos. And when they returned, Taylor went into the studio with Liz and Nathan and Borchetta to make her first album. On June 19, 2006, they released their first single from it: "Tim McGraw."

During the months they spent in the studio, Taylor took some time out to take driving lessons and after several failed attempts, she finally passed her driving test. A week later, while driving home to Hendersonville with Abigail Anderson sitting shotgun, she had the radio blasting and a girl called in to the station.

"I want to hear that Tim McGraw song," she said. "There's a lot of Tim McGraw songs, little darling, which one are you talking about?" the DJ on the radio asked.

"The one by Taylor Swift," the girl said. Taylor and Abigail screamed.

And Taylor almost drove off the road.

Pat Garrett heard it on the radio in Pennsylvania and blared his horn and rolled down his window and shouted "Home run!" as he drove along the country road toward his amphitheater. Everyone thought he was crazy, but he didn't care. He knew a good song when he heard it.

The single, "Tim McGraw," shot up to number 40 on the Billboard Hot 100 and number 6 on their U.S. list of Hot Country Songs.

Just before her album was released in October of 2006, Taylor went to Scott Borchetta, Nathan Chapman, and Rick Barker with a request.

"You ever hear of MySpace?" Taylor asked. "Yeah, it's that new thing—social media," Barker said.

"It's where the teenage girls go," Taylor said. "Can I create a page and get a few songs up?"

Barker looked at Borchetta and neither of them could disagree. "I like the way you think, "Barker said.

Taylor's first album, entitled *Taylor Swift,* was released on October 24, 2006. It generated five hit singles and launched her career in the United States. It became one of the twelve longest-running albums in the chart's fifty-seven-year history, selling over six million copies.

Although Rick Barker introduced Taylor to 500,000 fans, with the launch of her MySpace page, she doubled that.

She went on her first national tour for the album and every night after a performance, she stayed behind to meet her fans. It was more important to her than anything else. By the time the sun came up the next morning, there was still a line of teenage girls waiting for an autograph and a hug. It was a lesson she learned from LeAnn Rimes, who took her hand at her first concert.

TWENTY FIVE

The call from rapper and MTV producer Sway Calloway came in the middle of Taylor's 2007 tour for her first album, *Taylor Swift*. She had been opening for a number of country stars like Rascal Flatts, Kenny Chesney, Brad Paisley, and George Strait. Taylor and her best friend, Abigail, were in the studio where Taylor was working on her next album when she took the call from MTV.

"This is Studio A," she said answering the phone. "Taylor, what's up? This is Sway from MTV," came the reply.

"Hey, what are you doing?"

"I'm calling to let you know I have something really special planned for you." "Really?"

"I know you missed your high school prom last year because you were on tour, but I'm not gonna let that happen to you again this year. It's prom season, gorgeous! Since you're doing the road again this year, I found a school near one of your tour stops with a whole mess of single Southern boys who would love you to be their date to the prom!"

Taylor's eyes grew wide and she looked over at Abigail.

"Interested in giving one of these boys the biggest surprise of his life?" Sway asked.

"Stop playing around," Taylor said. "Are you serious?"

"I found a bunch of guys at Hillcrest High in Tuscaloosa, Alabama, who I thought would be pretty good matches for you."

Taylor gave Abigail a look and mouthed the words, *Oh my God...*

"Now we didn't tell them who the gal might be, but man, you are seriously their top pick for a dream date. I'm sending over a video of the fellas."

A big smile spread across Taylor's face. "I can't wait to watch," she said to Sway and said her goodbyes and hung up.

The studio engineer who had heard the whole thing grinned. "Happy?" he asked her.

Taylor could not stop smiling. "Ecstatic," she replied and turned to Abigail with a grin. "I finally get to go to the prom!"

Abigail cheered. "Finally! Good for you!"

In March, Andrea breezed into the living room waving something while Taylor and Abigail were watching TV. "Taylor, it has arrived," she said, waving a DVD. "Your future prom date." It was a disc of all the boys from Hillcrest High who did not have a date to the prom. When they made their proposal videos, they had no idea who their date might be, if they were so lucky to be chosen. All of them were asked to talk about themselves and state who they hoped their date would be. Beyoncé was mentioned, Jordan Sparks, and Carrie Underwood.

"They've got good taste in women," Taylor said. "I'm dateless," one boy came on camera and said.

"I don't have the money to buy a ticket," another said.

"Good solid reason," Taylor talked back to the TV. "I've just never had a girlfriend," yet another boy said. "I'm a nerd."

"Oooh, that scores points," Taylor said to Abigail.

Then a boy named Whit Wright came on and when they asked who he hoped it would be, he didn't hesitate. He said, "Please let it be Taylor Swift."

Taylor's heart melted as she watched him on her big screen TV.

"I just moved to this high school and I don't really know anybody," Whit said.

"It's so hard to move in your senior year," Taylor said, having moved around the country on tour her entire senior year.

"I'd like to take somebody," Whit continued, "but I couldn't find that special girl to take."

When all the boys presented themselves on video, it was time for Taylor to make the hard choice. She loved them all, so she and Abigail wrote their names on scraps of paper, crumpled them up, put them in a black top hat, and mixed them around. Taylor reached in and picked one and when she opened it up and saw the boy's name, she smiled broadly.

"Awesome!" she said, showing the scrap to Abigail.

"It was destiny," Abigail agreed.

When Mr. Hyche, the principal of Hillcrest High called Whit's name, announcing him the winner of MTV prom date contest, Whit thought he was going to faint. Mr. Hyche did it in front of the entire junior and senior classes in the gymnasium and when Whit walked up and stood next to his principal, everyone cheered and he instantly became the most popular guy in his school. "I'm the luckiest guy in the world right now," he said. "Man, I'm excited!" He couldn't concentrate in class; he spent the whole time imagining how Saturday night was going to go. Baseball practice wasn't much better. He was the starting shortstop and championships were coming up.

His jersey number was number 9.

Back at home in Nashville, Taylor stared intently at the rack of prom dresses hung across the wide doorway, separating the family room from the living room. She never had a problem picking a dress for any occasion, but this time it was unique. It was for an occasion she had no experience with: the prom. And it was not for her, it was all for Whit. "Picking a dress for prom is pretty critical," she said to Abigail going from a white gown to a yellow gown to a blue gown. She checked out the blue layered gown more closely.

"I love the color," Abigail said. "It's like a Cinderella dress."

"I can never pull off the layered look, so I'm passing on it," she said.

"That's my favorite," Abigail said.

Taylor heard that and stopped. "That's your favorite?" she asked.

"Yeah," Abigail said. She took it down and draped the straps over her neck and the dress hung down her front. "This is how I would wear it," she said and both girls giggled.

"Hey, if you like it so much why don't you wear it?" Taylor asked.

"You mean like outside?" Abigail asked.

"No, I mean like why don't you wear it and come to prom with me!"

"Oh, I don't know," Abigail hesitated.

"Hey listen. We've been best friends since ninth grade; we've never been to the same prom. Ever. Will you come to prom with me in Alabama?"

"You're asking me to the prom?"

"Not as my date but in my group. There are 39 other guys that do not have dates at that school. We'll just get there and find you one!"

The girls shared a laugh.

"So we're going to prom together..." Abigail asked. "YES!!"

After a lot of hemming and hawing, Taylor finally picked an elegant crème-colored gown. Abi would wear the blue.

On the Saturday afternoon of the prom for the Class of 2008 at Hillcrest High, Taylor and Abigail drove from Nashville to Tuscaloosa, Alabama, and showed up at Whit's house in her big white tour bus.

Whit stood out on his front lawn, anxiously waiting for his date to arrive. He wore a black suit with a pink vest and tie and held a huge armload of flowers, wondering who he was going to give it to. Abigail stepped off the bus first and let Whit know his date had arrived. And when Taylor stepped off, he almost fainted. It was his dream come true. He had prayed it would be her. They went inside and met his family and then they were off in her bus for their first stop of the day: the *Bama Belle,* a riverboat complete with working paddle wheel. They took a leisurely cruise up the Black Warrior River and ate a real Southern dinner.

"This is really, really good," Taylor said eating her last piece of fried chicken. "Be right back." She got up and went over to the table and filled her plate again.

"You are my kinda girl!" Whit said to her as she returned to their booth with her plate. Outside the window, Tuscaloosa's largest river motored by.

"So, like, who are your best friends?" she asked. "Wayne's probably my friend," Whit replied, not sure what she was getting at. "Does he have a date?"

Whit realized what was happening and shouted across the boat to his friend Wayne, who came over. Taylor and Abigail introduced themselves.

"You don't have a date, right?" Whit asked him and he shook his head. "Would you mind going with Abigail?"

Wayne was flabbergasted.

"This is my best friend. I brought her and we would love it if you would go with her," Taylor said.

"Oh! Oh, I-I was looking for a date," Wayne said. "You can totally join us," Abigail said, offering him a seat.

"Best friends going with best friends!" Whit said. After dinner, Whit and Taylor and Abigail and Wayne and a bunch of Wayne and Whit's friends returned to her tour bus for the ride to the prom. On the way, Taylor asked Whit why he was wearing a pink vest and tie.

"It is for Aunt Joan," Whit explained. "She's so committed to the baseball team and does so much for us—and then she got diagnosed with breast cancer and I love her to death, she's like my second mom—so, uh, I'm just wearing it for her."

Taylor was moved. "I love that's the reason why you chose pink," she said and got up. "Hold on a second." She hurried into the back and Abigail followed. When she came back, she had changed into a beautiful pink dress. "We have to wear pink tonight. For Aunt Joan," she said.

Whit was floored. It was incredibly thoughtful that she did that and it made him love and admire her even more.

Later, Taylor remarked, "It was such an unbelievable thing for him to do and I really, really wanted to join in and stand up and say something about it."

The Hillcrest Senior Prom was like a fairy tale, not only for everyone who came, but for Taylor and Abigail too. Taylor danced with all the other dateless boys who sent her their video, but she always returned to Whit. And when the night was over, she saved the last slow dance for Whit. "This was like a dream come true," he whispered to her as she danced. "Like a fairy tale."

Taylor was in heaven. When it was all over and she and Abigail headed back to Nashville, they talked. "This was the first time in over three years that I got to hang out with kids my own age," she said. "It was so much fun!"

Abigail agreed. "This was the most fun we have had in, like, forever!"

Taylor hugged her friend.

"Whit was a great guy," Abigail said.

"Totally," Taylor said. "We're playing here on the tour and I'm definitely going to look him up!" Then she closed her eyes and smiled. Tomorrow she would be back to the hard work of producing a new album and going on tour. But tonight—tonight was a fairy tale. They were elected king and queen of the prom and for everyone's kindness and friendship, she was eternally grateful.

Made in the USA
Middletown, DE
24 October 2020